PANZER III
VS
T-34
Eastern Front 1941

PETER SAMSONOV

OSPREY PUBLISHING
Bloomsbury Publishing Plc
Kemp House, Chawley Park, Cumnor Hill, Oxford OX2 9PH, UK
29 Earlsfort Terrace, Dublin 2, Ireland
1385 Broadway, 5th Floor, New York, NY 10018, USA
E-mail: info@ospreypublishing.com
www.ospreypublishing.com

OSPREY is a trademark of Osprey Publishing Ltd

First published in Great Britain in 2024

A catalogue record for this book is available from the British Library.

ISBN: PB 9781472860934; eBook 9781472860941;
ePDF 9781472860958; XML 9781472860965

24 25 26 27 28   10 9 8 7 6 5 4 3 2 1

Maps by bounford.com
Index by Rob Munro
Typeset by PDQ Digital Media Solutions, Bungay, UK
Printed and bound in India by Replika Press Private Ltd.

Osprey Publishing supports the Woodland Trust, the UK's leading woodland
conservation charity.

To find out more about our authors and books visit **www.ospreypublishing.com**.
Here you will find extracts, author interviews, details of forthcoming events
and the option to sign up for our newsletter.

Front cover, above:
A PzKpfw III Ausf. J moves past an emplaced T-34. The most vulnerable parts
of the T-34 were the vertical sides of the lower hull. In a defensive position,
these could be hidden by driving the tank into a tank trench or *caponier*. The
T-34 became harder to spot and harder to destroy, but its mobility was also
limited. A German tank platoon could combat such a defensive position by
'blinding' the T-34 with smoke and attacking from the side at close range.

Front cover, below:
A platoon of T-34 tanks drives into battle. This tank had no equal in its weight
class when it entered service, but its effectiveness in battle was hampered by
the poor organization of the Red Army in the summer of 1941. More often
than not, these tanks fought without support from infantry or artillery and
without adequate supplies of fuel and ammunition.

Title page:
A PzKpfw III tank navigates a bridge deployed by field engineers, 27 June
1941. The tank is pulling a trailer with two 200-litre fuel drums. Armoured
spearheads often outran their supply lines and could only rely on what they
carried themselves. (ullstein bild/ullstein bild via Getty Images)

Acknowledgements
The author would like to thank Bernhard Kast for his help with German-
language sources used in this book as well as Pavel Borovikov, Yuri Pasholok
and Artem Drabkin for photographs included in it.

Editor's note
Unless otherwise noted, all translations from the Russian are the author's own.
All degree measurements relating to armour are degrees from vertical, while all
those relating to climbing ability are degrees from horizontal. Both German
and Soviet tank designers used metric horsepower (PS), which is converted in
the text into kilowatts (kW) for clarity.

Glossary

ABTU	*Avto-bronetankovoye Upravleniye*, Automobile, Armoured Vehicle, and Tank Directorate, formed on 22 November 1934 to manage design and production of vehicles for the Red Army. See also **GABTU**.
Ausf.	*Ausführung*, 'implementation'. The suffix *Ausf.* followed by a letter was used to differentiate between German tank variants.
BT	*Bystrokhodnyi tank*, 'fast-moving tank'.
FAMO	*Fahrzeug- und Motoren-Werke*, Automobile and Engine Works.
Flak	*Fliegerabwehrkanone*, 'anti-aircraft gun'.
GABTU	*Glavnoye Avto-bronetankovoye Upravleniye*, Main Automobile, Armoured Vehicle, and Tank Directorate, formed from **ABTU** (q.v.) on 26 June 1940.
Kampfgruppe	A German battlegroup organized to carry out a specific mission.
KwK	*Kampfwagenkanone*, 'tank gun'.
MAN	*Maschinenfabrik Augsburg Nürnberg AG*.
MIAG	*Mühlenbau und Industrie AG*.
NKO	*Narodnyi Komissariat Oboronnoy*, People's Commissariat of Defence.
NKOP	*Narodnyi Komissariat Oboronnoy Promyshlennosti*, People's Commissariat of Defence Industry. This Soviet ministry was responsible for all military development until 1939 when it was dissolved into four separate ministries.
OKH	*Oberkommando des Heeres*, High Command of the German Army.
PaK	*Panzerabwehrkanone*, 'anti-tank gun'.
Panzertruppe	German tank troops.
Panzerwaffe	German tank forces.
PzKpfw	*Panzerkampfwagen*, 'armoured fighting vehicle'.
SdKfz	*Sonderkraftfahrzeug*, 'special purpose vehicle'.
SMK	A Soviet heavy tank named after Communist Party official Sergei Mironovich Kirov, assassinated on 1 December 1934.
Stavka	*Stavka verkhovnogo glavnokomandyvaniya*, Office of the Supreme Command. This was the most senior military council in the Red Army.
StuG	*Sturmgeschütz*, 'assault gun'.
TPU	*Tankovoye Peregovornoye Ustroystvo*, Tank Intercom Device.
Wa Prüf 6	Waffen Prüfen 6, 6th Department of the *Waffenamt* (German Weapons Office) responsible for the design of tanks.
Z.W.	*Zugfuhrerwagen*, 'platoon commander's vehicle'.

CONTENTS

INTRODUCTION

While no one could have predicted what a war between the Soviet Union and Nazi Germany would look like ahead of time, a well-informed observer could be certain that it would be a war of armour. The Soviet Union's Red Army quickly realized the potential of a mechanized force. Tank factories were among the most important facilities established when the Soviet government began its breakneck programme of industrialization in the late 1920s. The Large Kiev Manoeuvres of 1935 advertised the might of Soviet armour to the world; and tanks featured prominently in military parades held in Moscow's Red Square.

The Germans were more subtle. Prohibited from development of a wide variety of weapons under the terms of the Treaty of Versailles (1919), German arms giants continued to operate in secret through their foreign subsidiaries. Curiously enough, the Red Army ended up with a very good understanding of German tank development before the start of the Great Patriotic War (1941–45) as a result. Prototypes of the *Leichttraktor* light tank and *Grosstraktor* medium tank were tested in Kazan. Even after the German testing programme was terminated, Soviet forces captured a PzKpfw I Ausf. A light tank during the Spanish Civil War (1936–39). A PzKpfw II light tank was stolen in Nazi-occupied Poland in 1939 and a PzKpfw III medium tank was purchased from Germany in 1940. These tanks were studied and tested thoroughly, so that by June 1941 the Red Army had a fairly good idea of the composition and characteristics of German tank forces.

Conversely, the Germans knew next to nothing about the Soviet Union's newest armoured vehicles. The KV-1 heavy and T-34 medium tanks were developed in such great secrecy, that the only hint such tanks existed came in the form of the SMK heavy tank prototype (precursor to the KV-1) photographed by the Finns during the Winter War (1939–40). The Germans were only aware of the T-26 and BT-7 light tanks that

made up the core of the Soviet tank force, but these designs were already considered obsolete by the Red Army.

Despite not being prepared for the KV-1 and T-34 specifically, the German *Panzerwaffe* (armoured force) was already composed of combat veterans. German tank production also increased at a rapid pace. For example, only 51 PzKpfw III tanks were available for the invasion of Poland, most of which were experimental vehicles. Some 19 months later, at the start of Operation *Barbarossa* – the Axis invasion of the Soviet Union in late June 1941 – 1,440 PzKpfw III tanks were available, over 1,000 of which had improved guns and thicker armour to deal not just with the firepower of Soviet tanks that the Germans expected to see, but also with prospective threats.

By contrast, the Red Army was only just starting its major expansion. Confident that the Molotov–Ribbentrop Pact, signed on 23 August 1939, had bought him enough time, Stalin approved a modernization of the Red Army's tank forces that was expected to take several years. The vast majority of Soviet tank crewmen serving in 1941 had never seen combat, however, and a shortage of experienced instructors and NCOs meant that the lessons learned during the border clashes with Japanese tank forces at Lake Khasan (July–August 1938) and Khalkhin Gol (May–September 1939), the invasion of Poland and the Winter War were spreading slowly through the swelling ranks of Soviet tankers.

The PzKpfw III Ausf. A was the first step towards Germany's main medium tank. (Scherl/ Süddeutsche Zeitung Photo/ Alamy Stock Photo)

5

A typical 1940-production T-34. Note the night-fighting spotlight mounted on top of the gun mantlet. This feature was prevalent among Soviet tanks in the late 1930s, but had all but vanished by the end of the decade. Only the earliest T-34 tanks had the night-fighting spotlight. (Rossiyskiy Gosudarstvenniy Voyenniy Arkhiv)

Mastery of new tanks was also lagging behind. The T-34 had been in production for little more than a year by the time Operation *Barbarossa* began, and thus even commanders who were lucky enough to receive these brand-new tanks were reluctant to use them for training, meaning that the inevitable 'growing pains' were slow to surface and thus slow to be resolved.

The German invasion of the Soviet Union threw a sizeable spanner into the works of the modernization of the Red Army's tank forces. Deliveries of new tanks including the T-34 prioritized units positioned along the border, which were overwhelmed and destroyed piecemeal as German forces advanced into Soviet territory. Rather than building new tanks that suddenly became more important than ever, Soviet factories had to be dismantled and evacuated to safety vast distances away. In addition, the Red Army now had to raise an even larger cohort of raw recruits, having lost many of its experienced officers and NCOs. Nevertheless, the German steamroller heading east first slipped, then stalled altogether. Fortunes turned on the Soviet–German Front, albeit at a terrible cost as the Red Army began a counter-offensive at the gates of Moscow against a German force that the whole world had considered to be unbeatable only weeks before.

Among the tens of thousands of armoured vehicles that clashed in these vital months, two types stood out: the T-34 and PzKpfw III, both of which were chosen by their respective armies to be the backbone of their armoured force. Despite this, however, both had to share their glory with a sizeable proportion of supporting tanks; both were the subject of political intrigue, reflecting the people and systems that produced them; and both started out as much smaller and lighter vehicles but ended their service lives with thicker armour and more-powerful armament. This study explores the first months of the Great Patriotic War through the lens of a duel between these two formidable tanks.

CHRONOLOGY

1934
27 January   Wa Prüf 6 begins work on the Z.W. (*Zugführerwagen*), a replacement for the *Leichttraktor*.

1935
August   Z.W. prototypes are completed.

1937
April   Experimental batch of ten PzKpfw III Ausf. A tanks are completed.

8–9 April   Red Army ABTU prepares requirements for a next-generation medium tank based on combat experience during the Spanish Civil War.

1938
December   Production of the Z.W.38 (PzKpfw III Ausf. E) begins.

9–10 December   Designs of T-34 prototypes are presented to the Supreme Military Council of the Red Army.

1939
1 June   Trials of the A-20 tank begin.

2 July   Trials of the A-32 tank begin.

1 September   Nazi Germany invades Poland. World War II begins.

19 December   The T-34 is accepted into Red Army service.

1940
13 February   Trials of the A-34 tanks begin.

12 March   Two A-34 prototypes head to Moscow for demonstration to top Soviet government officials.

31 March   Design of the T-34 is approved for production.

June   Production of the T-34 begins.

1941
22 June   Nazi Germany invades the Soviet Union. The Great Patriotic War begins.

30 September   German forces draw closer to the Soviet capital. The battle of Moscow begins.

5 December   The German offensive on Moscow is stopped. The Red Army begins the offensive phase of the battle of Moscow.

Production of PzKpfw III tanks, 1940. This was the year when the PzKpfw III began its transition from a series of shaky prototypes to becoming the backbone of the *Panzerwaffe* (Heinrich Hoffmann/ullstein bild via Getty Images)

Tanks built at Factory No. 183. Left to right: BT-7; experimental A-20; T-34 typical of pre-March 1941; and T-34 produced between March and August 1941. (Rossiyskiy Gosudarstvenniy Voyenniy Arkhiv)

DESIGN AND DEVELOPMENT

PzKpfw III

During the 1920s, Krupp and Rheinmetall developed 8-tonne tanks codenamed *Leichttraktor* ('light tractor') that were secretly tested in the Soviet Union during 1930–32. It was clear that a new concept was needed and work on a heavier tank codenamed Z.W. (*Zugführerwagen* or 'platoon commander's vehicle') began on 27 January 1934. This tank kept the *Leichttraktor*'s 3.7cm Rheinmetall gun, but placed the driver's compartment and transmission in the front, fighting compartment in the centre and the engine in the rear.

Daimler-Benz and MAN each received a contract to build an experimental chassis while Krupp and Rheinmetall-Borsig were responsible for the turrets. MAN dropped out of the competition soon after. Two *Zugführerwagen* prototypes (Z.W.1 and Z.W.2) were completed in August 1935, both with Daimler-Benz hulls. While the layout was copied from the British Carden-Loyd VAE 393 tractor, the large roadwheels with an individual coil-spring suspension suggested some influence from J. Walter Christie's high-speed tanks. A 300PS (221kW) Maybach HL100 TR petrol engine gave the *Zugführerwagen* an impressive power-to-weight ratio. Other features, such as the turret, had many similarities to the German *Neubaufahrzeug* ('new construction vehicle') and *Begleitwagen* ('escort vehicle') tanks. The *Zugführerwagen* was heavier than originally estimated: 12 tonnes instead of 10 tonnes.

In April 1936 the *Zugführerwagen* was redesignated the PzKpfw III (3.7cm) and given the index SdKfz 141. An order for a batch of ten pilot tanks (PzKpfw III Ausf. A) was placed. These tanks, completed by April 1937, were even heavier: 15 tonnes. There were a number of changes compared to the Z.W.1 and Z.W.2 prototypes: the drive sprockets and idlers were smaller, the commander's cupola and gun mantlet were changed slightly and a deflector was added to prevent the turret machine guns from hitting the radio antenna when firing. The pilot tanks were powered by the weaker 250PS (184kW) Maybach HL108 TR petrol engine. Shock absorbers were added to the suspension to help deal with the worsening vibrations resulting from the tank's greater weight, although the fact that the idea of vertical coil springs was dropped after this variant suggests that they were not effective enough.

A second *Zugführerwagen* type was ordered in late 1935, shortly after the delivery of the first two prototypes. The Z.W.3 and Z.W.4 tanks both had leaf-spring suspensions. The Z.W.3 had eight wheels per side grouped into bogies; and two large leaf springs were used instead of individual coil springs. The Z.W.4 had a similar suspension, but it had three leaf springs: short ones in the front and rear and a full-length one in the middle. The Z.W.3 entered production as the PzKpfw III Ausf. B (2./Z.W.Serie), but the order was still conservative at 15 chassis: ten built as tanks and five as PzSfl III (sPaK) vehicles (a precursor to the StuG III assault gun). The PzKpfw III Ausf. B looked very similar to the PzKpfw III Ausf. A bar the suspension, but there was one other major visual change: the hatches in the front hull for servicing the brakes were round instead of square and had hinges. The PzKpfw III Ausf. B was once again heavier than its predecessor, weighing 16 tonnes. The ten tanks were completed and delivered by the end of 1937.

The Z.W.4 was put into production as the PzKpfw III Ausf. C (3./Z.W.Serie). This variant had the same square-shaped brake-maintenance hatches as the PzKpfw III Ausf. A, but there were other visual differences including a new driver's observation device and a commander's cupola from the PzKpfw IV Ausf. B with a 30mm-thick armoured ring. A variant with improved leaf springs entered

A PzKpfw III Ausf. D makes its way along a forest road, winter 1941/42. Tanks of this series still had an experimental leaf-spring suspension. (SA-kuva)

OPPOSITE

A PzKpfw III Ausf. E tank. While the PzKpfw III Ausf. A to Ausf. D were experimental vehicles built in small batches, the Ausf. E can be considered the first truly mass-produced variant. This was the first PzKpfw III to have six wheels per side with an individual torsion-bar suspension, as used on all subsequent variants of the vehicle. Production began in 1938 and the tanks were first used in combat against Poland in 1939. Even though superior models were available, PzKpfw III Ausf. E tanks were still in service for the invasion of the Soviet Union in June 1941.

production as the PzKpfw III Ausf. D (3b./Z.W.Serie), with the PzKpfw III Ausf. C retroactively changing to 3a./Z.W.Serie; 15 examples of the Ausf. C and 25 of the Ausf. D were ordered, with production completed in November 1938. In addition, five PzKpfw III Ausf. D were built instead of the five PzKpfw III Ausf. B tanks that were used to build assault guns. Production of these extra vehicles was completed in October 1940.

While these experimental tanks were being built, work was progressing on a revision of the *Zugführerwagen* concept, resulting in the Z.W.38. Instead of coil or leaf springs, it had a torsion-bar suspension that had already proved itself on the Swedish Landsverk L-60 light tank. Six individually sprung roadwheels were installed per side. The tracks were also different: rubber pads and lubricated track pins were designed to make driving on roads as smooth as possible. A 256PS (188kW) Maybach HL120 TR petrol engine and a ten-speed semi-automatic Maybach Variorex gearbox gave the Z.W.38 exceptional mobility for its class. Unfortunately, the sophisticated track links proved unreliable and had to be replaced with conventional metal ones; and the roadwheels quickly wore out at high speeds. Although the Z.W.38 was capable of reaching 67km/h, its top speed had to be capped at just 40km/h to prolong the lifespan of its running gear.

The Wehrmacht ordered production of the Z.W.38 – given the production index PzKpfw III Ausf. E (4./Z.W.Serie) – in much greater numbers than its predecessors: 759 on 11 June 1938, and 440 more on 6 December. Production got off to a slow start, however, with just one tank delivered in 1938 and only 50 by 1 September 1939. In total, 96 PzKpfw III Ausf. E tanks were built, 41 by Daimler-Benz and 55 by MAN.

A total of 435 tanks of the PzKpfw III Ausf. F (5./Z.W.Serie) variant were produced by Henschel, Daimler-Benz, MAN, MIAG, FAMO and Alkett. There were only a few visible changes: air intakes were added to the front of the hull to help cool the brakes; an observation port was added for the radio operator on the right side of the hull; and a *Nebelkerzenabwurfvorrichtung* ('smoke-grenade launcher') was mounted on the rear of the hull. The engine was replaced with the 265PS (195kW) Maybach HL120 TRM, which, unlike its predecessor, had impulse magneto ignition.

PzKpfw III Ausf. E

The Ausf. E and Ausf. F were also the first PzKpfw III variants to be fitted with improved main armour. The front and sides of the hull and turret were thickened from 14.5mm to 30mm, which was enough to withstand contemporary light anti-tank weapons, including the Polish 7.92mm Karabin wz. 35 and Finnish 20mm Lahti L-39 anti-tank rifles, and even low-velocity cannon such as the French 37mm SA 18.

The main armament of the PzKpfw III was upgraded when production of the PzKpfw III Ausf. G (6./Z.W.Serie) began in March 1940. This tank was initially very similar to the PzKpfw III Ausf. F, but in July 1940 the 3.7cm KwK L/45 was replaced with the 5cm KwK L/42. The campaign in France had shown that the 3.7cm gun could only penetrate the 40mm-thick armour of French tanks due to the armour's low quality, and even then only at close range. The new gun was much more powerful, and was capable of penetrating up to 75mm of armour. Although the old 3.7cm gun remained in production and service, older tanks were re-armed as supplies of the 5cm gun increased. Out of a total of 1,440 PzKpfw III tanks deployed by July 1941, 1,090 had 5cm guns.

Combat experience in Poland and France prompted the Germans to reinforce the tank's armour. The front hull armour was increased from 30mm to 60mm by the addition of appliqué armour. This was an effective way to protect the tank, but it came at a cost. The first of the new variants, designated the PzKpfw III Ausf. H (7./Z.W.Serie), 286 of which were produced until April 1941, weighed 21.8 tonnes and needed a reinforced suspension and 400mm-wide track links to compensate for the increased mass. A simpler design, the PzKpfw III Ausf. J (8./Z.W.Serie), entered production in March 1941. Instead of multi-layered armour, its front armour was composed of one 50mm-thick plate. The front of the turret was also reinforced to 50mm. The first tanks of this variant began to enter service just as Operation *Barbarossa* began. During 1941, 1,322 PzKpfw III Ausf. J tanks armed with the 5cm KwK L/42 gun were built.

It is important to note that due to parallel production and parts compatibility between series, it was common to see hybrid tanks. For instance, early-production PzKpfw III Ausf. J tanks were built with a PzKpfw III Ausf. H turret and some PzKpfw III Ausf. G tanks received a driver's observation device and commander's cupola from the PzKpfw III Ausf. F.

PzKpfw III Ausf. J

T-34

By the late 1930s the Red Army's armoured force was at a crossroads. Slightly improved by the use of sloped armour and appliqué armour plates, the T-26 light infantry-support tank had been in production since 1933; the T-46 was supposed to replace it, but was cancelled in 1938. The T-28 medium tank had only 30mm of armour and a short 76mm KT-28 gun that was capable of dealing with light field fortifications, but not enemy tanks; attempts to install a larger gun failed. The T-28 was supposed to be replaced by the T-29 medium tank, but this project was also cancelled in 1938.

The third tank in common use with the Red Army was the BT. The high mobility provided by the BT's Christie suspension and a series of powerful engines (first a copy of the Christie tank's Liberty engine, then the improved M-17 type) was deemed satisfactory. Requirements for a tank designated BT-20 were approved on 13 October 1937. In terms of protection, the BT-20 light cavalry tank was a step forward compared to the BT-7, with armour up to 25mm thick placed at an angle of at least 18 degrees. The BT-20 would be armed with a 45mm or a 76mm gun, just like its predecessor.

Requirements changed on 13 May 1938, however. The BT-20 now needed to have up to 30mm of sloped armour, and also a gun mantlet thick enough to withstand fire from 37mm guns. A fourth crewman was also added. He would sit in the hull and operate the BT-20's radio and a 7.62mm DT machine gun.

On 21 August 1938, NKOP (People's Commissariat of Defence Industry) order #335ss instructed Factory No. 183 in Kharkov to produce three experimental tanks: one with a convertible drive and two with only tracks. The design for these tanks was presented on 27 August 1938. Instead of a distinct break in the tank's silhouette, the front armour was composed of one sharply sloped plate. The sides were also sloped. This tank was now referred to as the A-20 rather than BT-20. As requested by the NKOP, a variant with tracks was also presented. This tank was called A-20 (tracked). Dropping the convertible-drive mechanism saved nearly 1 tonne of weight compared to the basic

The A-20 tank was based on the BT series concept with its four roadwheels per side and convertible drive. The hull was widened to allow for a radio operator/hull gunner to sit next to the driver. (Rossiyskiy Gosudarstvenniy Voyenniy Arkhiv)

The A-32 tank was a departure from the A-20, featuring five roadwheels per side instead of four and no convertible drive. Unlike the A-20, this A-32 also has a 76mm gun. (Rossiyskiy Gosudarstvenniy Voyenniy Arkhiv)

A-20 tank. In this early concept, the weight saving was used to increase the ammunition capacity from 160 45mm shells to 200 and 48 7.62mm machine-gun magazines to 58.

The two projects quickly diverged. ABTU Chief Dmitriy G. Pavlov's report to the Supreme Military Council of the Red Army, made on 9 December 1938, already described the tracked design as having a 76mm gun while the convertible-drive design retained a 45mm gun. The name of the vehicle also changed. At first the word *gusenichniy* ('tracked') was shortened to just 'G', making the designation of the prototype A-20G. Later, the tank received an entirely new designation: A-32.

The designs continued to diverge. Although the A-32 was supposed to be lighter than the A-20, even with the extra ammunition, the decision to use a 76mm gun instead of a 45mm gun made it heavier than its convertible-drive sibling, which retained the 45mm gun. The A-32 also had slightly thicker armour at 30mm, whereas the A-20's armour thickness remained at 25mm. The fully loaded A-20 now weighed 18 tonnes, but the A-32 weighed 19 tonnes.

This was not the end of the A-32's transformations. Trials had shown that the 500PS (368kW) V-2 diesel engine was more than sufficient for a vehicle of this weight. As a consequence, in July 1939 Pavlov ordered an investigation into the possibility of increasing the A-32's armour. Preliminary calculations showed that increasing the armour thickness all-around by 10mm would increase the weight of the A-32 to 19.5–19.6 tonnes. Pavlov gave the order to build an A-32 with 45mm-thick armour all-around. Trials with a second A-32 prototype loaded to a weight of 24 tonnes showed that the V-2 engine could deal with this extra weight.

A contract for two tanks with 45mm-thick armour was signed on 28 September 1939. This new tank received the designation A-34. On 19 December 1939 decree #443ss marked the acceptance of a number of new vehicles into service, including the improved A-32. The final variant of the tank with 45mm of armour and a new 76mm F-32 gun would be designated T-34.

At the time this decree was signed, the two A-34 prototypes were still in the early stages of assembly. The first prototype was delivered to the Red Army on 10 February 1940, with the second following two days later, and trials began on 13 February. The two tanks had a 2,500km-long course ahead of them, including 300km of driving on paved roads, 1,000km on dirt roads and 1,200km off-road. Special obstacle trials were also conducted. Other components such as the 76mm L-11 gun (used as a replacement for the F-32 until production of the latter was under way) and 71-TK-3 radio coupled with the TPU-2 intercom were also tested.

While the mobility of the A-34 proved satisfactory, the Red Army requested many changes to be made to the gun mount. The radio was deemed to be satisfactory, enabling communication between the two tanks at ranges of up to 18–20km, even in motion. The biggest problem with the radio was its location. As it was placed in the turret bustle, it had to be operated by the commander (who also doubled as the gunner), which distracted him from other tasks. The Red Army requested that the radio be moved to the hull and operated by the hull gunner. Additionally, a TPU-3 instead of a TPU-2 intercom should be used.

Having received the military's seal of approval, it was time to present the two A-34 prototypes to the Soviet government. Marshal Voroshilov ordered that the tanks not be transported from Kharkov to Moscow by train, but make the drive of some 800km under their own power. A convoy comprising the two tanks and a Voroshilovets tractor carrying spare parts set out on 12 March 1940. Owing to snowy conditions and longer-than-expected maintenance halts, the three vehicles were more than a day late, arriving in Moscow at 1745hrs on 17 March.

Even though the original programme called only for driving from Kharkov to Moscow and back, the two tanks made a detour to the NIBT (Scientific Institute for Armoured Equipment) Proving Grounds at Kubinka on 24 March. Senior officials gathered to observe how the tanks' 45mm-thick armour dealt with modern anti-tank guns. A 37mm Bofors gun taken from a Finnish Army Vickers Mark E Type B light tank captured during the Winter War and a 45mm Model 1934 gun used in a BT-7 tank were employed for the trials, with the first A-34 prototype chosen as their target. Each gun fired two shots from a range of 100m. The 37mm gun could not penetrate the A-34's armour, but destroyed the left-side observation device. The 45mm gun could not penetrate the armour either. A shot to the side of the turret only left a dent, although a shot that hit the welding seam between the turret bustle floor and turret side resulted in spalling that damaged a mannequin placed inside the tank. This shot also jammed the turret, although the jam was cleared by the crew with the help of a jack. These trials showed that the A-34 could indeed resist fire from modern anti-tank weapons, although more thorough trials would be conducted in the future.

Agreements to begin production of the A-34 were concluded during 29–31 March 1940. The two tanks departed for Kharkov at 0130hrs on 2 April and arrived at Factory No. 183 at 0900hrs on 10 April. They remained in use for testing while Factory No. 183 got to work setting up production of the tank.

Even though decree #443ss described the T-34 as an A-32 with thicker armour and an F-32 gun, the tanks that were first assembled in June 1940 were very different vehicles. F-32 production lagged behind schedule and the gun was not available until January 1941. The first T-34s were stuck with using the L-11 gun. Another difference was the driver's station. Rather than having a cabin, the driver on the production T-34 received his own hatch that was flush with the front of the hull. The hatch had one periscope inside it and two more on the flanks, giving the driver a combined range of vision of 127 degrees. Outside of combat, the hatch could be locked open to make it easier for the driver to see where he was going.

OPPOSITE

An early-production T-34. Tanks similar to this example were built between June 1940 and March 1941.

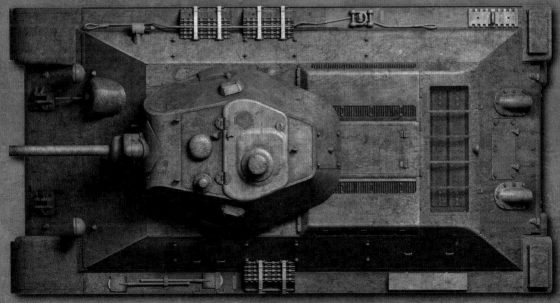

An A-34 tank undergoing Molotov cocktail trials. This tank looks like a T-34, but there are several differences, one of the most prominent being the driver's cabin. (Rossiyskiy Gosudarstvenniy Voyenniy Arkhiv)

There were also major changes to the turret. The initial turret used on the two A-34 tanks was too narrow. Factory No. 183 was asked to find more room for the crew without sacrificing the slope of the armour plates or widening the hull. This was achieved by changing the geometry of the turret, giving an extra 160mm of width for the fighting compartment. These wider turrets (only 38 narrow-width turrets were built) can be distinguished by a rectangular patch of armour below the pistol port.

Another major change resulted from measures taken to accelerate production. The turret made up of rolled plates welded together was complicated to assemble, so a cast turret was developed to simplify the production process. Trials showed that cast armour was slightly weaker than rolled armour, however, and so the cast turret had nominally 52mm-thick sides (due to the imprecision of the casting process, the thickness could vary between 51mm and 55mm) to offer equivalent protection to the 45mm-thick rolled plates. This increased the turret weight from 1,885kg to 2,035kg.

The hull was also changed to simplify production. Originally, the whole front hull was made from one large curved piece of armour. Shaping such a large and thick piece of armour was time-consuming, and so a simpler solution was developed by which the upper and lower front plates were cut separately and connected with a 100mm-thick cast beam. The beam was welded to the hull plates and the weld seam was reinforced with rivets. Trials showed that this joint withstood repeated hits from 45mm and 76mm guns. This composite hull was put into production in June 1940. The rivets were later removed as the welding was considered sufficiently strong. A fully cast front hull was also designed, but never produced.

Another major change had to do with the radio. Work to find an acceptable location for the radio began after the first trials of the A-34, but nowhere had been found by the time T-34 production started. A compromise was reached: the T-34 would be built with a radio in the turret and Factory No. 183 would refurbish existing tanks at its own cost once a way to fit the radio into the hull was found. Experiments began in August 1940 but only finished on 14 October 1940. Trials of five T-34 tanks fitted with 71-TK-3 radios in the hull to the right of the bow gunner showed that the tanks could communicate at ranges of 18–19km while moving in third or fourth gear or up to 26km when stationary.

OPPOSITE

A typical T-34 produced after March 1941. Of note are the cast turret, which was easier to produce than the welded type, a longer and more powerful 76mm F-34 gun, and the absence of a backup commander's periscope in the turret hatch.

18

LATER-PRODUCTION T-34

A typical pre-war production T-34. Changes included a new 76mm F-34 gun, cast turret and cast connecting beam separating the upper and lower front hull plates. Note the presence of a PTK periscope at the loader's station. This periscope was nearly identical to the commander's PT-4, but it was not linked to the gun. (Rossiyskiy Gosudarstvenniy Voyenniy Arkhiv)

Large-scale trials of T-34 production tanks were held during October–December 1940. Three September–October production tanks were selected and run through trials of 2,706km (132 hours 27 minutes), 2,571km (120 hours 35 minutes) and 2,680km (129 hours exactly) respectively. The trials report acknowledged that the T-34 had much room for improvement. A number of changes were requested, including the installation of an improved 76mm F-34 gun and 600PS (441kW) V-2K diesel engine, and an increase of the tank's lifespan to 7,000km or 250 hours of operation. Some of the desired changes were implemented on the existing T-34, while others were postponed for implementation on the T-34M tank that was expected to replace the T-34 in production by the end of 1941. Owing to the Axis invasion, however, this never took place.

The T-34 continued to evolve during 1941, the most notable change being the introduction of the F-34 gun. This gun not only had improved ballistics compared to the L-11, but was also more reliable. The last of 286 T-34 tanks armed with the L-11 gun was produced in March 1941.

Another component of the T-34 tank that evolved throughout 1941 was the driver's hatch, which was vulnerable to jamming and damage. The hatch was sealed to be airtight to resist Molotov cocktails, and splash protection strips were added around the edges. In August an entirely new hatch flap entered production. It was made of 60mm-thick cast armour with a thick flange instead of 45mm rolled armour. Instead of one periscope in the middle of the hatch, there were now two with overlapping fields of vision. Both periscopes were equipped with armoured shutters. The driver could close one in combat and operate the T-34 by looking through the other. If that periscope was damaged, he could switch to a second one and replace his back-up. The right-hand periscope offered a field of vision of 95 degrees, the left 85 degrees (the range of the latter periscope was partially obscured by the tank's fender). The two periscopes installed around the driver's hatch were removed.

These and other changes were introduced into the T-34 gradually without discrete breaks in series, making attempts to split production by year (Model 1940, Model 1941, etc.) or type (T-34A, T-34B, etc.) pointless. The close attention paid to maintaining parts compatibility meant that both newly built and refurbished T-34 tanks could be visually different depending on where and when their components were built.

TECHNICAL SPECIFICATIONS

Several production series of the PzKpfw III were in service at the time of the Axis invasion of the Soviet Union and the tank continued to change over the course of the next several years, both to meet new threats and adapt to its changing role on the battlefield. This chapter describes the most advanced model of the PzKpfw III tank available on the front lines during the battle of Moscow (September 1941–January 1942), the PzKpfw III Ausf. J.

The T-34 entered production in June 1940. Even though production was not divided into multiple discrete series, the design remained in flux throughout the Great

A T-34 tank stuck after ramming a PzKpfw II tank, August 1941. Even though the T-34's F-34 gun could effortlessly dispatch this light tank, shortages of 76mm ammunition often left Soviet tankers with no other weapon except this desperate manoeuvre. (Daily Mirror Library/ Mirrorpix/Mirrorpix via Getty Images)

Patriotic War. Specifications differed based on the factory and year (or even month) of production. Owing to careful attention paid to parts compatibility, a T-34 could be built with a turret, hull and running gear all from different factories, resulting in a large number of visually distinct variants being fielded throughout the Great Patriotic War. This chapter describes a typical T-34 built with parts produced at Factory No. 183 that would be commonly encountered in late 1941.

LAYOUT

The hull of the PzKpfw III followed the same layout for all German tanks of the period. It consisted of a tub with a superstructure in the middle, which formed the turret platform. The front of the hull formed a complicated shape to make room for the Maybach SSG 77 transmission. The transmission was located in the front and the engine in the rear, with a shaft connecting the two running under the fighting compartment. Two crewmen, the driver and the radio operator/hull gunner, sat in the front of the hull. The commander sat below the cupola and behind the gun. The loader and the gunner flanked the gun. Observation ports for the latter two crewmen were cut into the front half of the side and large hatches with two flaps in the rear half. The front flap had another observation port; the rear flap had a pistol port. These hatches were used by the loader and the gunner to enter

A mock-up of a T-34 showing the layout of the fighting and engine compartments, Park Pobedy, Moscow. The driver and radio operator/hull gunner sat in the front of the hull with the commander/gunner and loader behind them on seats suspended from the turret ring. (Author)

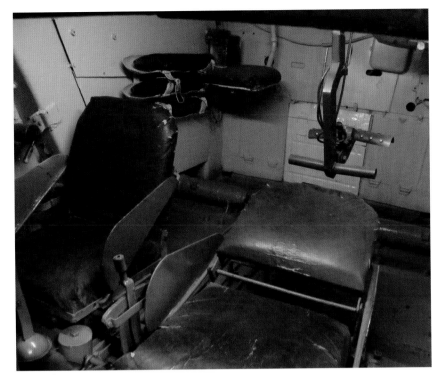

A closer view of the T-34's crew compartment. This tank, on display at Patriot Park, Kubinka, lacks the ammunition crates that made up the floor of the fighting compartment. The loader's seat (left rear) and commander/gunner's foot rest (right rear) can be seen behind the seats of the radio operator/hull gunner (left front) and driver (right front). (Author)

and exit the tank. Two more pistol ports were cut into the rear of the turret and covered by conical plugs when not in use. Evacuation hatches were cut into the sides of the hull. These came in handy, because the driver and radio operator entered the tank via the turret.

While the T-34's layout was reminiscent of those of its ancestors, the BT tanks, it was greatly simplified. The upper hull was in the shape of a bisected pyramid, providing sloped armour on every side. While the lower front and rear plates were also sloped to improve protection, the lower sides still had to be vertical in order to accommodate the roadwheels. As in the BT tanks, the driver sat in the front of the tank. Since the T-34 had a radio operator/hull gunner in the driver's compartment, the driver and his hatch were located in the front left corner with the other crewman to his right. The turret and fighting compartment were located right behind them. The engine compartment was located behind the fighting compartment, separated by a firewall. The transmission was in the very back of the tank.

The T-34's turret sat towards the front of the hull on a turret ring with an inner diameter of 1,420mm. Three pistol ports (one in each side and one in the rear) were available for close defence. When not in use, the pistol ports were sealed with a conical plug. The T-34 commander sat to the left of the gun. Because there were only two crewmen in the turret, the commander also performed the duties of a gunner, aiming through either a periscopic or a telescopic gun sight. The loader sat on the other side of the turret from the commander. In addition to loading the gun, the loader's role included servicing the coaxial 7.62mm DT machine gun. On some tanks, the loader used the same periscope as the commander/gunner.

PzKpfw III Ausf. H, Musée des Blindés, Saumur. In addition to the appliqué armour installed on this variant, this particular tank has been retrofitted with additional spaced armour on the front of the hull. This tank already has the 5cm KwK 38 L/42 gun, a considerable improvement over earlier PzKpfw III variants' 3.7cm gun. (Author)

FIREPOWER AND ARMOUR

The PzKpfw III's armament consisted of a 5cm KwK 38 L/42 gun with a coaxial MG 34 machine gun in the turret and a second MG 34 in the hull. In total, 78 rounds of fixed ammunition for the gun were carried in the hull: 22 in a bin at the rear of the fighting compartment on the right side; 24 in a bin on the left side; 14 on the left side of the engine compartment, accessible through a door in the bulkhead; two in a bin on the bulkhead; eight on the left wall of the fighting compartment; and eight more under the commander's seat. In addition, 4,950 rounds of ammunition for the two machine guns were carried in 33 150-round belts spread between bags hanging on the left and right walls of the fighting compartment.

The PzKpfw III's front turret armour was 50mm thick and angled at 15 degrees, although early tanks of this series still had older turrets with 30mm-thick armour. The rounded gun mantlet was 50mm thick. An observation port (covered with an armoured shutter when not in use) was cut into the right side of the turret. The sides and rear were also 30mm thick and angled at 25 degrees and the rear at 12 degrees respectively. The roof of the turret was 10mm thick. The front half was angled at 85 degrees and the rear was horizontal. A commander's cupola with 50mm-thick walls was installed towards the back of the roof. There was a hatch covered by a pair of 10mm-thick flaps in the top for use by the commander.

The PzKpfw III's lower front hull plate was 50mm thick and sloped forwards at an angle of 22 degrees. Above it was a small plate that was also 50mm thick, sloped backwards at an angle of 55 degrees. This plate housed the tank's headlights as well as ventilation openings for the final drives. The plate above the transmission was 25mm thick and nearly horizontal at an angle of 85 degrees. Two hatches for servicing the transmission were cut into this plate. The front of the superstructure was also 50mm

OPPOSITE

The 5cm KwK 38 L/42 gun was installed in PzKpfw III tanks starting in July 1940. This gun had greater armour penetration than the 3.7cm gun used on early PzKpfw III tanks, but it still turned out to be insufficient for fighting T-34 and KV-1 tanks encountered in 1941.

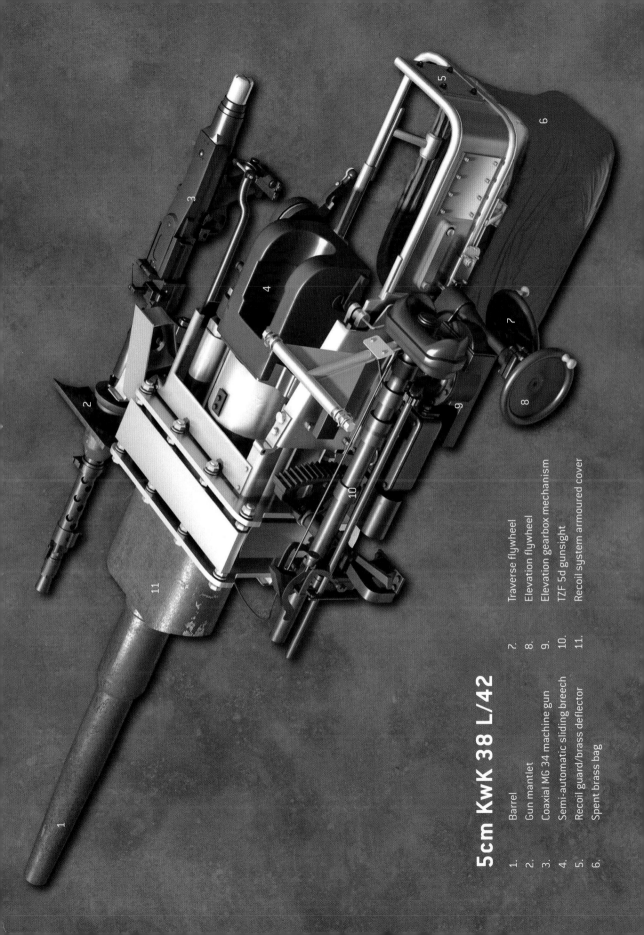

5cm KwK 38 L/42

1. Barrel
2. Gun mantlet
3. Coaxial MG 34 machine gun
4. Semi-automatic sliding breech
5. Recoil guard/brass deflector
6. Spent brass bag

7. Traverse flywheel
8. Elevation flywheel
9. Elevation gearbox mechanism
10. TZF 5d gunsight
11. Recoil system armoured cover

German sub-calibre armour-penetrating shot consisting of a lightweight sabot carrying a tungsten-carbide core. (Author)

OPPOSITE

The 76mm F-34 gun was used in T-34 tanks from March 1941 until the T-34 was phased out in favour of the T-34-85 in 1944. The F-34 was an exceptional weapon for its time, delivering both a potent high-explosive shell and an armour-piercing shell that allowed it to fight any contemporary tank at long range.

thick but sloped much less radically at an angle of only 10 degrees. This plate housed the MG 34 machine gun in a Kugelblende 50 ball mount with a hemispherical gun shield and a Fahrersehklappe 50 driver's vision device. The vertical sides of the hull and superstructure were 30mm thick. The horizontal superstructure roof was 10mm thick and the slightly sloping engine deck (the front half was angled at 85 degrees, the rear 77 degrees) was 15mm thick. The rear armour had a complex shape just like the front. Plates 30mm thick were presented at angles of 15 degrees (top), 10 degrees (middle) and 65 degrees (bottom).

The T-34's F-34 gun was located in the centre of the turret. The gun mount afforded it depression to -5 degrees and elevation to +28 degrees. A coaxial DT machine gun was installed to the right of the F-34. A second DT was installed in a ball mount on the right side of the upper front hull plate and operated by the hull gunner, but he could observe the battlefield only through the sight of his machine gun.

The T-34 carried 77 rounds of ammunition for the gun. Three rounds were stowed horizontally on the left turret wall and six on the right; the remainder were spread between eight bins located on the floor. The rubberized lids of the bins made up the floor of the fighting compartment. The T-34 also carried 3,906 rounds of ammunition for the machine guns in 62 63-round magazines. On tanks without a radio, the extra space was used for 13 additional magazines. The turret bustle accommodated 16 magazines, making it easier for the loader to reload the coaxial DT machine gun.

The T-34's turret armour was 45mm thick all-around if welded armour was used and 52mm thick if it was cast. The sides and rear were angled at 30 degrees and the front was rounded. The roof of the turret and hull was 15mm thick. The 40mm-thick upper sides of the T-34 were sloped at an angle of 40 degrees. A 45mm-thick vertical plate with four cut-outs for suspension arms (the front wheel on each side lacked a cut-out) made up the lower hull. Each suspension arm was accompanied by a bump stop. A 20mm-thick horizontal plate ran above the tracks and formed a floor for the pannier. The front of the T-34's hull was composed of 45mm-thick rolled upper and lower plates sloped at an angle of 60 degrees, with a rounded 100mm-thick cast connecting beam between them. A large cut-out was made for a driver's hatch on the left side of the upper front plate. The 60mm-thick hatch flap contained two observation periscopes in quick-release slots. Each periscope was protected by an armoured shutter. The rear of the hull also featured sloped armour. The lower rear armour was fixed in place, but the upper rear armour was held on with two hinges.

German tank ace Otto Carius described the T-34 and its F-34 gun as 'magnificent', 'universally feared' and 'a threat to every German tank up until the end of the war' (Carius 2020: 10). Even the PzKpfw III's 50mm surface-hardened front armour was no match for the T-34's gun. In trials held against captured tanks, firing at this kind of armour from a range of up to 800m and an angle of 20 degrees resulted in large

76mm F-34

1. Barrel
2. Gun mantlet
3. Coaxial DT machine gun
4. Semi-automatic sliding breech
5. Recoil guard/brass deflector
6. Brow pad

7. Elevation flywheel
8. Elevation gearbox mechanism
9. TMFD-7 gunsight
10. Trunnion
11. Recoil system armoured cover

breaches with a diameter of 90–100mm. On the second hit, the German plate cracked in half. High-explosive shells fired from 800m could breach the PzKpfw III's side armour or knock the commander's cupola clean off.

The armour of earlier PzKpfw III tanks (30mm with another 30mm-thick plate welded on) fared no better. As with the monolithic armour, a large breach (110–165mm in diameter) formed on the first hit at a range of 900m and an angle of 20 degrees. On the second hit the plates shattered. A hit with a high-explosive shell fired under the same conditions blew out the roof of the turret platform. Hits to the PzKpfw III's side armour resulted in breaches up to 400mm in diameter. Penetration trials at longer ranges were not conducted, but extrapolations showed that even the toughest armour of the PzKpfw III could be penetrated at a range of nearly 2,000m.

Meanwhile, the PzKpfw III's KwK 38 L/42 gun had a much harder time against the T-34. German manuals show that an 'honest' penetration of its opponent's front hull armour was impossible. If firing head-on, PzKpfw III gunners were instructed to aim for weak points (machine-gun ball, gun recuperator or driver's vision port) in order to damage the T-34 somehow. It was also possible to aim at the small section of the turret face where the armour was nearly vertical. This part of the T-34's turret could be penetrated at ranges of 100m or less with the 5cm PaK 38 towed anti-tank gun. The PzKpfw III's weaker 5cm KwK 38 was less useful. Generalmajor Willibald von Langermann und Erlencamp, commander of the 4. Panzer-Division, noted: 'Our 5cm KwK tank guns can only penetrate weak spots in very specific conditions at very small ranges, up to 50m. Our tanks can be penetrated at a range of hundreds of metres' (quoted in Ulanov & Shein 2013: 160). The reality was not quite so grim however, because a lucky shot could penetrate the T-34's side and rear at ranges of up to 500m. Nevertheless, until PzKpfw III variants armed with the longer 5cm KwK 39 L/60 and tungsten-carbide armour-piercing shot became widely available in 1942, there was little recourse but to aim at the T-34's turret ring and try to jam it, or attempt to hit the T-34 from the side at uncomfortably close range.

Segment cut out of a T-34 tank, T-34 Tank Museum, Russia. While the armour plate was 45mm thick, placing it at an angle of 60 degrees gave it a line-of-sight thickness of 90mm. (Author)

MOBILITY

The PzKpfw III was powered by a Maybach HL120 TRM petrol engine, which produced 265PS (195kW) at 2,600rpm and 300PS (221kW) at 3,000rpm. The engine was connected to a transmission with a Zahnradfabrik SSG 77 six-speed (plus one reverse) gearbox and a differential turning mechanism. Top speed was limited to 40km/h, as the running gear could only withstand higher speeds for a very short time. The running gear consisted of six double roadwheels 520mm in diameter with an individual torsion-bar suspension and three return rollers 310mm in diameter per side. The first and last wheel on each side had a hydraulic shock absorber. Each track consisted of 93–94 (depending on the degree of track wear) identical track links. Each link was 400mm wide at the pin, but narrowed to 360mm to slot into the next track.

The PzKpfw III carried 320 litres of petrol inside a single fuel tank in the engine compartment, which was enough for 155km of driving on a paved road, 115km on a dirt road or 85km off-road.

A captured PzKpfw III Ausf. H during obstacle trials. The PzKpfw III had a weaker engine, narrower tracks and worse traction than the T-34, giving the latter a considerable advantage in off-road mobility. (Tsentralniy Arkhiv Ministerstva Oborony Rossiyskoy Federatsii)

The V-2 engine, T-34 Tank Museum. This 500PS (368kW) V-12 diesel provided the T-34 with unprecedented mobility. (Author)

The T-34's gearbox allowed for four speeds forward and one reverse. At 1,700rpm, the V-2 engine developed normal power of 400PS (294kW). Maximum speed at this power was 48.30km/h forward and 6.90km/h in reverse. At 1,800rpm the engine produced 500PS (368kW) and the T-34 could achieve a speed of 53.85km/h. The engine could idle at as low as 600rpm and accelerate to 2,050rpm.

Assembled T-34 track segment, Kubinka Technical Centre. Coupled with the powerful V-2 engine, the T-34's wide tracks gave it superior off-road mobility compared to other contemporary tanks. (Pavel Borovikov)

The T-34's upper rear armour could be flipped open to extract the transmission. A small maintenance hatch was cut out in the centre of the plate to allow easier access when extraction of the transmission was not required. Final drives were housed in two bulges in the lower rear plate. A pin gear with rollers on the pins to reduce friction made up the drive sprocket. In addition to the idler and drive sprocket, five wheels were installed on each side, with the gap between the second and third being slightly larger than the rest. A total of 72 550mm-wide track links were used per side, 36 with a guide horn and 36 without. Each of the upper side plates had attachment points for two external fuel tanks with a total capacity (assuming four fuel tanks carried) of 134 litres of diesel.

The powerful V-2 diesel engine was one of the most impressive features of the T-34, and one that the Germans took note of. Indeed, the engine allowed the T-34 to develop a considerably higher top speed than the PzKpfw III, even without pushing the engine to its limit. The economy of the engine also bestowed a considerable advantage. The T-34 carried enough fuel to travel almost twice as far as the PzKpfw III without refuelling: 300km compared to 155km on a paved road and 250km compared to 115km on a dirt road.

The superior engine power of the T-34 also helped it when overcoming natural and artificial obstacles. In trials conducted against packed-snow walls 1.7m high and 4m thick, a captured PzKpfw III Ausf. H took seven minutes and five attempts to penetrate the first wall. It took a total of eight attempts and 16 minutes to penetrate two of the walls. The T-34 used in the trials penetrated three walls on the first attempt. The total time taken to overcome this obstacle was just ten seconds.

Early-model T-34 with a 76mm L-11 gun negotiating an anti-tank trench during trials, spring 1941. The T-34's wide tracks with good grip and the powerful V-2 engine allowed it to climb the toughest slopes. (Tsentralniy Arkhiv Ministerstva Oborony Rossiyskoy Federatsii)

The T-34 showed a superior ability to negotiate trenches as well as walls. The obstacle in this trial consisted of a relatively easy downward slope that ended in a steep 3m-high wall. Neither the T-34 nor the PzKpfw III was capable of navigating the obstacle unassisted (nor could the Matilda III or Valentine II tanks that also took part in the trials). The T-34 equipped with grousers managed to climb out of the trench if one fascine was thrown in first. The PzKpfw III was unable to get out even with the use of four fascines.

The T-34's superior engine power also allowed it to sweep aside a strip of fortifications made up of two layers of Czech 'Hedgehogs' (anti-tank obstacles made from girders welded together). The PzKpfw III was also able to navigate through the layers of 'Hedgehogs', but it took longer to do so. An attempt by the PzKpfw III to ram straight through the layers failed and the driver had to back up and carefully move the individual 'Hedgehogs' aside in order to pass through safely.

The T-34 also showed superior mobility when driving in regular snow. During the aforementioned trials, the PzKpfw III was unable to climb a 13-degree slope even after it was cleared of snow. In the same conditions, the T-34 was able to climb a 15-degree slope that had not been cleared. The T-34's wide tracks allowed it to move in snow up to 1.8m deep. The tank would sink to a depth of 42cm, but could still be driven in first gear.

The climbing ability of the PzKpfw III was generally limited due to its narrow tracks and their poor traction. Trials showed that the tank slipped on a dry 35-degree incline, even if it had sufficient engine power to allow it to complete the climb. The maximum incline the PzKpfw III could overcome was 30 degrees. The T-34 could climb a slope of 38 degrees.

VISION AND COMMUNICATIONS

One of the greatest advantages of the PzKpfw III over its contemporaries was not its gun or its armour, but the presence of a commander who could dedicate his full attention to surveying the battlefield. Although he had no rotating periscope and had to twist his body around in a confined space to change his field of view, he still had a 70-degree field of view, albeit without magnification. The T-34's commander/gunner observed the battlefield through his 2.5× PT-4-7 periscope with a 26-degree field of view. An auxiliary periscope in the turret hatch offered him a 120-degree field of view to the right and the fixed periscope in the side of the turret gave a 90-degree field of view to the left. Despite lacking periscopic magnification, the PzKpfw III's commander had a wider field of view available to him without having to swap between different devices.

The two loaders had a similar number of vision devices. The T-34's loader looked through a fixed periscope that offered a 90-degree field of view to the right. Similarly, the PzKpfw III's loader had an observation slit that offered him an 80-degree field of view.

The primary vision device available to the PzKpfw III's gunner was the Leitz 2.4× TZF 5d monocular telescopic sight that offered a 25-degree field of view. The T-34's commander/gunner could use his PT-4-7 periscope to aim the gun or switch to the

TMFD-7 telescopic sight that offered the same 2.5× magnification, but only a 15-degree field of view. He had the advantage of being able to combine 360-degree vision with handling the gun, meaning that he did not have to hand off a target he spotted, but also had to do two crew members' jobs. A T-34 commander/gunner could either look for a target or engage one, but not both at the same time.

It is often claimed that the quality of Soviet gun sights was inferior to that of German sights, but contemporary evaluations do not support this theory. British wartime reports commend the quality of Soviet gun sights. Light transmission was high: 26.3 per cent for the periscopic sight and 39.2 per cent for the telescopic sight, compared to just 20.1 per cent for the German 2.4× TZF 5b telescopic sight. The Americans also had a high opinion of the T-34's gun sights, even calling them the 'best in the world' and 'incomparable to any sights currently known or under development in America'. (TsAMO RF F.38 Op.11355 D.1712 L.93) Nevertheless, a good gun sight only helps if the gunner had already spotted the target. Until then, the PzKpfw III had an advantage and could very well withdraw if it could not engage the T-34 on favourable terms.

Another advantage held by the PzKpfw III was its radio equipment. While the range of the FuG 5 was less than that of the T-34's 71-TK-3, the German set was much more widely fitted. This meant that every PzKpfw III was able to remain in radio contact with the rest of its platoon. Meanwhile, only 40 per cent of all T-34 tanks were built with radios prior to 1943. If a 71-TK-3 was fitted, the T-34's hull gunner operated it. If necessary, the commander could patch into it directly through the TPU-3 intercom. The T-34 platoon commander could remain in communication with his superiors at a longer range (over 20km vs 6.4km by voice), but the only ways of communicating with his subordinates were by visual means: signal flags, flares and tracers. This meant that T-34 tanks would have to remain within line of sight of each other in order to maintain combat effectiveness as a unit, whereas PzKpfw III tanks could split up and stay in contact.

Two vision diagrams composed by Engineer-Major L.S. Tolokonnikov for *Vestnik Tankovoy Promyshlennosti* (Armoured Industry Journal), 1944. At left is a 1941-production T-34; the 360-degree observation provided by turret periscopes and gun sights is not shown. At right is a PzKpfw III Ausf. H; the vision provided by gun sights and pistol ports is not shown. The vision provided by the PzKpfw III commander's cupola is marked in red on the top-down view to avoid confusion. Note that not every observation device provided its full range of vision without movement of the head. (Author)

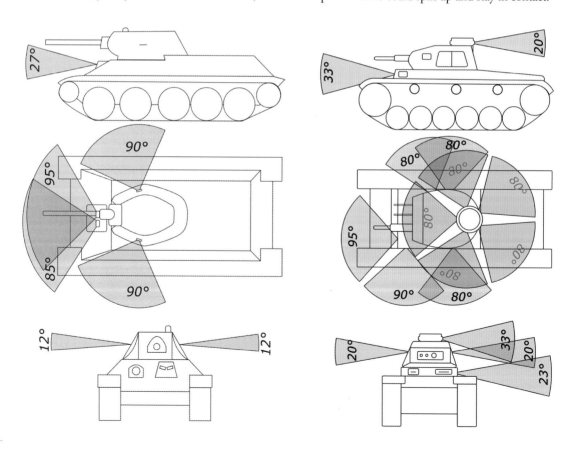

THE COMBATANTS

GERMAN ARMOUR ORGANIZATION

After nearly two years of combat in World War II, the organization of German forces was well established by the start of Operation *Barbarossa*. The structure of the armoured division was created in 1935. The Wehrmacht built each Panzer division around two tank regiments and one regiment of motorized infantry. Unlike the Red Army, the German Army stressed the importance of infantry and supporting units in these divisions. The engineering organization was expanded in 1938 and another regiment of infantry added after that.

Following the campaigns in Poland and France, the organization changed again. Now the Panzer division had one tank regiment of two battalions. Each battalion had one company of PzKpfw III and PzKpfw IV medium tanks and two companies of PzKpfw II light tanks. The artillery assets were also reinforced. Because some Panzer divisions were upgraded from light divisions (armed only with the PzKpfw I and PzKpfw II) and others were tailor-made for specific missions, the exact numbers and types of tanks could differ. Panzer divisions equipped with Czech PzKpfw 35(t) and PzKpfw 38(t) light tanks also had slightly different compositions. In addition, by 1941 some Panzer divisions featured an extra tank battalion. As a result, while the weakest Panzer division (9.) had only 135 tanks, the strongest (7.) had 258. These numbers do not include PzKpfw I tanks that had been excluded from tank regiments and given to the division's sappers.

The Panzer division's tanks were supported by an impressive amount of artillery: 24 10.5cm light howitzers, 12 15cm heavy howitzers, four 15cm heavy infantry guns, 20 7.5cm light infantry guns, 30 8cm mortars and 48 3.7cm PaK and 5cm PaK 38 anti-tank guns. The tanks were also supported by about 6,000 men in the infantry units.

The Panzer division also had a large number of wheeled vehicles – 561 cars, 1,402 trucks and 1,289 motorcycles – to transport its men and supplies. Additional vehicles in excess of the authorized amount were also common. The Panzer division also included 44 armoured cars (chiefly in the reconnaissance battalion) and between 109 and 115 half-tracks. The half-tracks are often forgotten when comparing Soviet and German tank divisions, but this is a serious mistake. A T-26 Model 1931 tank with twin turrets each mounting a 7.62mm DP light machine gun was no more useful on the battlefield than a PzKpfw I light tank or SdKfz 251 half-track with similar armament. Arguably, the ability of the latter vehicle to carry a squad of infantry made it even more useful. The SdKfz 251 could also be armed with a more substantial weapon like a 3.7cm PaK, making it more than a match for Soviet light tanks. The 2cm KwK 30 and KwK 38 autocannons mounted on vehicles such as the SdKfz 222 armoured car also posed a major threat to light tanks like the T-26, which were only expected to resist rifle bullets.

On average, a Panzer division had 182 tanks in its regiments, and a few dozen armoured vehicles that could face Soviet light tanks as equals. An average Red Army tank division with 111 tanks in each of its two regiments was about equal in terms of raw tank numbers, but lacking in everything else. The Panzer division had twice as many motorized infantrymen, twice as many light howitzers, five times as many light infantry guns, two-thirds more medium mortars, and an incomparably higher number of cars, trucks and half-tracks. The greatest artillery advantage was in anti-tank guns. The Red Army tank division had no anti-tank assets of its own at all. As practice showed, the motorized rifle divisions of the mechanized corps could not be relied upon to fill that gap.

German tank crewmen gathered around their immobilized PzKpfw III, winter 1941/42. The tank's narrow tracks, poor traction and low power-to-weight ratio limited its off-road mobility in winter. (Arthur Grimm/ullstein bild via Getty Images)

The number of heavy guns was close: 12 Soviet 152mm howitzers to 12 German 15cm heavy howitzers, plus four 15cm heavy infantry howitzers. Considering the Red Army's shortages of artillery tractors, however, the German heavy howitzers enjoyed far greater mobility on the battlefield.

The Wehrmacht's greatest advantage over the Red Army was not in the number of tanks or riflemen. The Germans had the luxury of being able to hone their organization and refine the equipment of their armoured divisions through two relatively short-lived campaigns. Hitler saw the need to expand the Wehrmacht before the invasion of the Soviet Union and he had plenty of time to do so. Expansion of the number of tank and motorized infantry units was ordered by the OKH on 26 September 1940, although some began to form sooner than that. Rather than break up cohesive units, established Panzer divisions each 'donated' one regiment of their tanks to newly forming Panzer divisions; a relatively quick way to expand the motorized force. Even though individual Panzer divisions lost some of their striking power, the German Army as a whole remained healthy and even the most lagging Panzer divisions were ready for battle by the spring of 1941.

PzKpfw III Ausf. A during training exercises at Wünsdorf, November 1938. (dpa picture alliance/Alamy Stock Photo)

LUDWIG BAUER

Ludwig Bauer was born on 16 February 1923 in Künzelsau, Baden-Württemberg. As his father and grandfather were both officers, Bauer had little doubt about his career path. After a brief stint in the *Reichsarbeitsdienst*'s Arbeitsgruppe 354 during September–November 1940 he was posted to Reserve-Panzer-Abteilung 33, stationed at Sankt Pölten-Spratzern. The four months he spent there were allocated to basic training as well as the study of PzKpfw I, II, III and IV tanks. Basic training was followed by gunner training at a tank school in Putlos.

In August 1941, Bauer volunteered for active service. He was sent to Panzerjäger-Abteilung 521, armed with Panzerjäger I tank destroyers, where he took the role of commander of one of the four PzKpfw II light tanks attached to the battalion to protect the tank destroyers, since he had prior experience with tanks.

Bauer first encountered the T-34 at Mtsensk on 11 October 1941. He remembered the situation well, as he was outside of his tank at the time delivering a report and armed only with a pistol. In his experience, the appearance of the T-34 changed everything and turned the Soviet tank forces into a serious threat. In later battles, he learned that the PzKpfw III's 5cm gun was helpless against the T-34 even at close range, but the PzKpfw IV armed with a long 7.5cm gun could confidently knock it out at a range of up to 800m.

Bauer's toughest battle in Operation *Typhoon* was not Mtsensk, but Tula. His unit neared the city in late November 1941. He recalled powerful defences surrounding the city, including a massive anti-tank trench. A wave of German tanks rushed to beat Soviet guns and fill the trench with fascines made from demolished log houses. His PzKpfw II advanced in the second wave alongside the motorized infantry. Bauer's tank climbed a hill so close to the city that he could make out the lights of tramcars. Deprived of cover, the tank was hit by Soviet anti-tank guns and caught fire. The driver and radio operator were killed, but Bauer successfully baled out. His wounds included a shell splinter in an eye and several shards in one of his hips. Bauer was taken back to Yasnaya Polyana for treatment, then further back from the front lines to Orel.

Two weeks later he was well enough to be transported to Grünberg, Silesia (modern-day Zielona Góra, Lubusz Voivodeship), and after a four-week-long recovery at home he returned to the 3. Kompanie/Reserve-Panzer-Abteilung 33 for three weeks of officer-candidate training. Bauer was eager to get back to his comrades on the front line, but upon completion of the training, he was sent to a different unit. Bauer returned to the Eastern Front as a gunner in a PzKpfw III in Panzer-Regiment 33, 9. Panzer-Division. His tank was a new variant armed with the 5cm KwK 39 L/60 cannon.

As a tank gunner, Bauer took part in the offensive on Voronezh in June 1942. He experienced near-constant fighting, even at night, mixed together with heavy labour carrying petrol canisters (lorries were forbidden from approaching the front line) and maintenance duties. Pervitin (a form of methamphetamine developed in Germany) was issued to compensate for lack of sleep.

On 28 June, Bauer's tank was knocked out, killing the rest of the crew aside from him and radio operator Sepp Lackner.

THE GERMAN TANK CREWMAN

Prior to the Third Reich, the German Empire practised conscription with a mandatory two- or three-year conscription term and ten years in the reserves. Article 173 of the Treaty of Versailles abolished this practice, but it was reintroduced in 1935 when Hitler shrugged off the restrictions of the treaty. Men aged 18–45 (55 in Prussia) could be conscripted for a period of two years, with the exception of Jews, Catholics who had taken holy orders and various categories of criminals.

Much like the Soviet conscript, a German's introduction to the Army began at a school age. Paramilitary training was conducted through units of the Hitlerjugend (Hitler Youth) organization. A course with a motorized unit of the Hitlerjugend

Bauer and Lackner's new PzKpfw III was destroyed by a KV-1 a week later. The company commander assigned them to another PzKpfw III together, but this tank was destroyed on 24 August. Bauer was wounded once again, but lightly. He returned to service only a few days later. After serving with Panzer-Regiment 33 until the end of February 1943, Bauer returned to study at Sankt Pölten, where his officer training began.

On 1 March, Bauer was promoted to *Unteroffizier* and then to *Fahnenjunker* on 1 April. He continued his training at Wünsdorf and then Groß Born (modern-day Borne Sulinowo). *Fahnenjunker* training consisted of military science and leadership courses in addition to the study of armament and *matériel*. Upon completion of these courses, Bauer became an *Oberfähnrich* on 1 July, but that was not the end of his studies. Immediately upon promotion, he began company commander courses in Berlin and graduated as a *Leutnant* on 1 October.

Bauer returned to Panzer-Regiment 33 as a platoon commander in the 3. Kompanie, this time with a PzKpfw IV. His promotion to an officer did not harm his luck, as he successfully cheated death at Krivoy Rog twice, on 10 and 12 January 1944 – the sixth and seventh times Bauer had survived the destruction of his tank. After celebrating his 21st birthday on the front line, Bauer and the 9. Panzer-Division were withdrawn to Vienna and then Nîmes to re-form. The division was still training when D-Day came on 6 June, and so it was only deployed westward on 27 July. On 6 August, the division arrived at Alençon and engaged units of the Third US Army. The 9. Panzer-Division was recalled once again to Sankt Pölten at the end of August. The 2. and 3. Kompanien of Bauer's battalion received new PzKpfw IV tanks, but the 1. Kompanie that Bauer assumed command of on 4 December had *Sturmgeschütze*.

In his *Sturmgeschütz*, Bauer fought at Bastogne in January 1945. This was where he began to suspect that there was no way to win the war. In his opinion, the Americans might not have fought as well as the Red Army, but they had better weapons, particularly artillery. Bauer's *Sturmgeschütz* was knocked out on 11 March, after which he was reassigned to command a small group of Panther medium tanks that were gathered for a counter-attack at Erndtebrück. His Panther was hit by mistake on 6 April by a 'friendly' Hetzer tank destroyer and caught fire. Bauer thought that his luck had run out because the Panther's hatch was blocked by a camouflage net, but the net burned up quickly and he was able to escape.

Panzer-Regiment 33 was disbanded on 16 April 1945. Surviving troops split up into small groups and tried to slip through enemy lines. Bauer came across a farmhouse, where civilians treated the burns he had sustained when baling out from the Panther and handed him over to the Americans. He spent a year in POW camps, where he learned that he had been awarded the Knight's Cross for his fighting at Iserlohn in April. During his career, Bauer earned the Knight's Cross of the Iron Cross, Iron Cross 1st Class, Iron Cross 2nd Class, silver tank combat badge, gold wound badge, and the Winter Warfare on the Eastern Front medal.

After his release, Bauer returned to his home town. His status as a cavalier of the Knight's Cross helped him get a job with Opel. He later joined the Bundeswehr reserve and retired in the rank of *Oberstleutnant* in 1975. He died on 20 May 2020 in Künzelsau, Baden-Württemberg.

generally provided 80 hours of driving time and 105 hours of mechanic training. Ideally, after leaving the Hitlerjugend, a prospective tank crewman would move on to the NSKK (*Nationalsozialistisches Kraftfahrkorps*, National Socialist Motorized Corps) in which he would continue his studies as a driver or a mechanic, but this was not always the case. The RAD (*Reichsarbeitsdienst*, Reich Labour Service) also provided paramilitary training. Men aged 18–20 were given paramilitary training by the SA (Assault Detachment) even after the 'Night of the Long Knives' in mid-1934 when the SA was purged and the power of the organization diminished.

Training over the course of the first year of military service was aimed at developing the soldier's physical and mental capacity in order to make him a *vollwertiger Kämpfer* ('fully capable fighter') with the support of more experienced soldiers. During the second year, the goal was to train the soldier as a *selbstständiger*

German tank crewmen, including one standing on a PzKpfw III, warm themselves at a fire, November–December 1941. (Arthur Grimm/ullstein bild via Getty Images)

Einzelkämpfer ('independent fighter'). During this year, the soldier also mastered his speciality and promising troops received supplemental training to become NCOs.

Unlike the Red Army, which would routinely thrust a conscript into a company of unfamiliar soldiers, the German system was based on the concept of *Wehrkreise* (military districts). Recruits were drawn from the district where a particular division was based. This assignment was persistent, and even sick or wounded soldiers returned to the same division after recovery if possible.

Once assigned to a division, the conscript would complete basic training as a part of the division's replacement battalion. Future tank crewmen followed the same six-month basic training course as the infantry. In general, the Germans urged tank and anti-tank crews to train closely together so that each group understood the strengths and limitations of the other. The value of combined arms in general was emphasized. To that extent, training during the first year involved training on foot including marching drill and use of the pistol, rifle, grenades, a machine gun for fighting when dismounted and the 3.7cm PaK. Unlike the infantry, future tank crewmen would learn the strengths and limitations of armoured vehicles, including how to disable them.

The recruits would be split up according to their speciality. Around 40 out of 100 men would be chosen to be gunners, 30 as tank drivers, 15 as radio operators and 15 as wheeled-vehicle drivers. The actual content of the training depended on what vehicles were available for the unit. For instance, PzKpfw I drivers would also serve as auxiliary radio operators. If PzKpfw III or IV tanks were available in the unit, some men selected as gunners would first be trained as loaders in these tanks. There was also some amount of cross-training; for example, drivers received basic instruction on firing the weapons in the PzKpfw I and PzKpfw II. Note that these proportions were established according to regulations published in 1938, when very few PzKpfw III and IV tanks were available.

Specialist training was both theoretical and practical. Lessons from military campaigns were integrated into the training programme quickly. Recruits were trained by officers with combat experience gained during the campaigns in Spain, Poland and France specifically so that the mistakes of those campaigns would not happen again. Tank troops would receive 21 weeks of training at the tank school in Münster or in Wünsdorf.

SOVIET ARMOUR ORGANIZATION

Following the Soviet campaign in Poland and the introduction of new tank types, the Red Army's mechanized corps were disbanded and re-formed into new mechanized (later tank) corps. In 1941, each consisted of two tank divisions, one motorized infantry division, one motorcycle regiment, two corps artillery regiments, one signals battalion, one battalion of motorized engineers and even an air wing.

The tank division consisted of 63 KV heavy tanks, 210 T-34 medium tanks, 48 light tanks and 54 chemical (flamethrower) tanks: 375 tanks in total split between two tank regiments, each with one KV battalion, two T-34 battalions and one battalion of chemical tanks. Tank divisions also had a three-battalion motorized rifle regiment and an artillery regiment. This made for about 3,000 riflemen accompanying the tanks plus 12 152mm howitzers, 12 122mm howitzers, four 76mm regimental guns, 12 37mm anti-aircraft guns and 18 82mm mortars.

The motorized rifle division contained two motorized rifle regiments, one tank regiment, one artillery regiment, one reconnaissance regiment, one anti-tank gun battalion and one battalion of 37mm antiaircraft guns, plus support units. This gave the motorized rifle division approximately 6,000 fighting men plus 12 152mm howitzers, 16 76mm guns, eight 37mm anti-aircraft guns, 12 82mm mortars and 60 50mm mortars.

In theory, the full-strength mechanized corps fielded 1,031 tanks, 546 of which would have been new types (T-34 and KV), plus 172 cannons of all types, 186 mortars, 5,161 cars, 352 tractors and 1,679 motorcycles. Out of the more than 36,000 men, about 9,000 were riflemen. In practice, however, the compositions of the mechanized corps were somewhat poorer. Out of 22 mechanized corps available as of June 1941, just two (the 1st and 6th) had over 1,000 tanks, for an average of 555 tanks per corps. The situation with new tanks was even worse: no mechanized corps had even close to the authorized amount; the 4th and 6th were the closest with 416 and 352 vehicles respectively. Over one-third of the mechanized corps had no new tanks at all. On average, there were only 114 KV and T-34 tanks per mechanized corps, with the rest made up chiefly of T-26 and BT tanks. Three of the mechanized corps had fewer than 100 tanks – less than one-tenth of the authorized amount – and no new tanks at all.

The number of old tanks alone does not accurately represent the state of these corps. Some of the BT and T-26 tanks had seen a decade of service and required work to keep running. Out of 12,223 tanks available to the Red Army in the Soviet Union's western military districts, just 2,145 were in the first category, meaning that they were brand new and ready for service. The majority of tanks, 7,900 vehicles, were in the second category, requiring light repairs that could be carried out by the crew provided they had the parts. A total of 1,199 tanks were in the third category and 979 in the fourth, meaning that they were in need of an overhaul at regional workshops and repair factories respectively. Spare parts for these tanks simply did not exist.

The transition from old types of tanks to new ones meant that insufficient quantities of parts were delivered for both. No parts for M-17 or V-2-34 engines were delivered at all, while 25–30 per cent of tanks urgently needed new tracks, which could not be provided. These defective tanks would have to remain in service for years to come, as the Soviet Union's industry at its pace in 1941 would only produce enough tanks to bring its new mechanized corps to authorized strength by the end of 1943. Replacement of obsolete tanks with new models could only start then. At that point, the BT series would make room for the T-34, the KV-1 would be replaced with the KV-4 or KV-5 and the T-26 would be replaced by a new infantry-support tank, potentially the T-50. At the start of the Great Patriotic War, a replacement for the T-26 had not yet been decided.

Consumables were also in short supply; for example, out of 550,000 76mm armour-piercing shells ordered in 1940–41, only 146,000 had been delivered by 1 June 1941. Ammunition and fuel were also largely stored centrally. In peacetime, mechanized corps had only one or two loads of fuel and ammunition on hand. There were also shortages of wheeled transport, tracked prime movers and motorcycles. Much like the tracked vehicles, a considerable percentage of wheeled ones were inoperable due to a lack of spare tyres; and existing tyres were heavily worn.

The staffing situation was equally poor. Not a single mechanized corps reached authorized strength. Just six mechanized corps, less than one-third, counted over 30,000 men; three had fewer than 20,000. On average, a mechanized corps had just 26,500 men – a far cry from a full fighting force.

Individual tank divisions within the same mechanized corps could also vary widely in strength. For instance, the 8th Tank Division of the 4th Mechanized Corps was relatively well staffed, but the 32nd Tank Division of the same corps was in a disastrous state. Out of 58 authorized senior officers, the division had only 29, 110 junior officers out of 621, 897 NCOs out of 2,166, and just seven out of a total 69 authorized medical personnel.

The Red Army was well aware of its manpower problems in its new mechanized corps and was rapidly trying to resolve them, but it was no easy feat to grow the numbers of tankers from 90,000 in 1938 to 650,000 in 1941. This process was delayed by a lack of experienced personnel and training facilities. Although some officers and NCOs were transferred from existing tank units and already had experience with armour, this was not always the case. These new personnel were not evenly distributed. For example, the 17th Mechanized Corps reported that some of its units were filled entirely with raw recruits conscripted in the spring of 1941.

Newly formed mechanized corps and tank divisions set up up living quarters, organizing shooting ranges, ordering manuals, training aides and turning new recruits into soldiers and seasoned soldiers into NCOs. All of this took time. For example, the aforementioned 17th Mechanized Corps estimated that its battalions would reach full cohesion by September 1941. Around the same time, Zhukov expected the 7th Mechanized Corps of the Moscow Military District, a corps that began forming in the summer of 1940, to be ready for practical exercises that would allow the General Staff to refine the composition of the mechanized corps and the tactics they would use. By this metric, one could expect newly formed mechanized corps to complete cohesion exercises by mid-1942 at the earliest. Even mechanized corps with a lower percentage of fresh conscripts were not in a much better state by the start of the Great Patriotic War.

A typical T-34 built in mid–late 1941. This particular tank already has the F-34 gun introduced in March 1941 and tow hooks typical of wartime-production T-34 tanks, but does not yet have the driver's hatch with two vision periscopes. The rivets reinforcing the connecting beam between the upper and lower front plates are also indications of an early-production T-34. (Author)

The men with prior experience among these tank divisions were unlikely to be experienced with the T-34 tank. Production was ramped up slowly, and even though 960 T-34 tanks had been issued by the end of June 1941, 402 – almost one-half of the total – only left the factory in May or June. This means that some of the Soviet tankers who went into battle on 22 June 1941 would have received their tank mere weeks or even days prior. The Red Army was stuck in the unenviable position of having to fight with inexperienced tank crews that had to learn the ins and outs of their tanks on the battlefield or die trying.

The same T-34 from the rear. This tank still has a rectangular transmission maintenance hatch and a removable rear turret plate for extracting the F-34 gun without having to remove the entire turret. (Author)

THE SOVIET TANK CREWMAN

The first decrees mandating service in the Red Army were made in 1918. Mandatory military service was enshrined into Soviet law in 1925. Conditions and duration of service were modified several times before the Great Patriotic War; and the criteria for service were expanded in 1935 in response to Nazi Germany officially shrugging off the restrictions of the Treaty of Versailles. The 1936 Constitution of the USSR, adopted on 5 December that year, declared that 'the defence of the Motherland is a sacred duty of every citizen of the USSR'. There were still some exemptions for service: members of the 'exploiting classes' (children of former nobility, Tsarist officers and bourgeois), Cossacks, kulaks, clergy, the children of poor families and orphans. Students could also defer their service until the completion of their education. The conscription age was lowered from 21 to 19.

This changed on 1 September 1939. A new law titled 'On general duty of service' was passed, removing all prior restrictions. Now, military service was the duty of all male Soviet citizens. Deferments were given to those with infirm parents and criminals serving prison sentences. A service term for privates was set for two years starting on 1 January after their conscription, and three years for NCOs. Upon completion of their service, privates and NCOs remained in the reserve until the age of 50. Women with specialized medical, veterinary and technical backgrounds could also be conscripted.

Preparations for service in the Red Army would begin in school. Two hours per week were dedicated to preliminary military training in grades 5–7 and pre-conscription training in grades 8–10 and post-secondary institutions (with the exception of post-secondary students who had already completed military service). Before starting their military service, students would already know the basics of the

Soviet recruits studying the design of tank armament. This appears to be a relatively well-equipped classroom, but not all conscripts recruited in 1941 had the luxury of such training. (Istoriko-Memorialniy Muzeyniy Kompleks Bobriki)

organization of the Red Army and its role in Soviet society. More practical training included physical fitness (including swimming and skiing), hygiene, first aid, marching drill and navigation. Older students learned the basics of marksmanship, first with small-calibre rifles and then military rifles, the use of hand grenades and defence against chemical warfare.

Voluntary pre-military training at OSOAviaKhim (Society of Cooperation with Defence, Aircraft and Chemical Construction) could also be conducted. Through this organization, Soviet citizens that passed a series of physical tests would be awarded achievement badges, including the prestigious 'Ready for Labour and Defence' (GTO) for general fitness and 'Voroshilov's Marksman' for marksmanship with a rifle. The OSOAviaKhim could also train students for specialist roles in the Red Army, although the quality and availability of this training could greatly vary by region.

Once conscripted, Soviet tankers would undergo 1,400 hours of training over the course of ten months. All tank crewmen went through political, tactical and physical training in addition to specialized tank training. The duration of training depended on the specialty. For example, a tank driver received 100–120 hours of classroom instruction on driving, while other crewmen received only 15–30 hours. Tank drivers would also spend 15 hours driving light tracked vehicles (tractors or tankettes) and ten hours driving light tanks. Owing to the relative scarcity of medium and heavy tanks, only five hours of driving would be completed with such vehicles. Other tank crewmen would take a condensed version of the course consisting of 15 hours of driving tracked vehicles, and three hours in a tank.

Senior Lieutenant Dmitry F. Lavrinenko (far left) and one of his tank crews. Lavrinenko is credited with knocking out 52 enemy tanks during his short career. (Wikimedia/Public Domain/Unknown)

DMITRY FEDOROVICH LAVRINENKO

Dmitry F. Lavrinenko was born on 14 October 1914 in the Cossack village of Besstrashnaya in Krasnodar Krai. After completing school, he studied to become a teacher. He volunteered for service in the Red Army and joined its ranks on 1 November 1934. Initially allocated to the cavalry branch, he later enrolled in the tank school in Ulyanovsk.

Lavrinenko began the Great Patriotic War as a platoon commander with the rank of lieutenant in the 15th Tank Division of the 16th Mechanized Corps. This corps was poor in *matériel*, being equipped with fewer than one-half of its authorized number of tanks. The division chiefly fielded obsolescent BT tanks with a handful of T-28 tanks formerly belonging to the 14th Heavy Tank Brigade. Only about 30 per cent of the corps' vehicles were in fighting shape at the start of the Great Patriotic War, and all Lavrinenko's unit could do in the first days was withdraw to the east. Contemporaries recall that his tank broke down along the way, but he refused orders to scuttle it. His crew managed to keep the tank limping long enough to break out of the encirclement at the battle of Uman. Lavrinenko's stubbornness may have saved his life, as a considerable part of the 15th Tank Division could not break out and was destroyed.

Surviving tankers were reorganized into newly forming tank brigades. Personnel from the former 15th Tank Division were allocated to the 4th Tank Brigade, including Lavrinenko. The 4th Tank Brigade began to form on 19 August 1941 at Prudboy, just west of Stalingrad. The brigade received 22 T-34 tanks built at the Stalingrad Tractor Factory and seven KV-1 tanks built in Chelyabinsk when the order was given to move to Kubinka. There, the brigade received the rest of its vehicles: 31 BT-5 and BT-7 tanks. Lavrinenko was lucky to end up with a T-34.

In October 1941, Lavrinenko finally had a chance to even his score with the Germans. The 4th Tank Brigade was defending positions at Perviy Voin, south-west of Mtsensk. His first mission consisted of supporting the brigade's motorized infantry battalion that came under attack by elements of the 4. Panzer-Division on 6 October. Lavrinenko's platoon of four T-34 tanks made the best of their vehicles' mobility advantage by emerging from behind a hill, striking quickly and disappearing again, only to appear elsewhere a short time later. This tactic yielded results and Lavrinenko claimed four enemy tanks in this engagement, successfully withdrawing with wounded infantrymen carried on his engine deck and no losses among his tanks.

Individual tactical successes like these did not stop the German advance, but at the very least they slowed the invaders down, making an opening for additional raids. Over the next few days, Lavrinenko's platoon made good use of tank ambushes. A combination of thorough camouflage and dummy tanks built from logs allowed his tankers to attack and withdraw without losses. By

Owing to the scarcity of motor vehicles and the sudden start of the Great Patriotic War, Soviet tankers would likely have had considerably less practical experience than required in the summer of 1941.

Gunners received as much as 315 hours of instruction on firing a tank gun, while a tank driver would receive as little as 50 hours. Radio operators would spend as much as 270 hours on the topic of radio communication, while other tankers devoted just 30 hours to this task. A tank commander required 240 hours of additional instruction delivered over the course of his ten months.

The Red Army also filled in for education that soldiers might not have received before being conscripted. Troops who were illiterate or barely literate would take night classes to bring them up to speed. Soldiers who did not speak sufficient Russian would learn the language instead of taking part in some of the political training or study of

11 October, his crew had claimed seven enemy tanks destroyed. The front line continued to move east, and by this time the 4th Tank Brigade retreated to Mtsensk, taking a place in the second line of defence of the 50th Army. The total number of kills scored by Lavrinenko in the fighting for Mtsensk is unknown, but various sources credit him with up to 17 enemy tanks destroyed. What is certain is that his performance in the defence of Mtensk was exceptional. Major-General Dmitry D. Lelyushenko, the commander of the 1st Special Guards Rifle Corps that the 4th Tank Brigade was attached to at Mtsensk, compared Lavrinenko and his men to the soldiers of the Imperial Russian Army who had fought Napoleon's forces here some 150 years previously.

Soon after, on 16 October, the 4th Tank Brigade received orders to return to Kubinka. Lavrinenko's tank was left behind, temporarily assigned to the 50th Army to guard its headquarters. On his way to catch up with the 4th Tank Brigade, he was delayed by a traffic jam caused by a stream of refugees and retreating Red Army units. When he reached Serpuhkov, the tank and its crew were commandeered by garrison commander Colonel (later Lieutenant General) Pavel A. Firsov. Firsov received news about an approaching German vanguard, but he had no resources to counter it, aside from the single T-34. Lavrinenko set up another successful ambush, returning to Serphukov with a wealth of trophies including an anti-tank gun and a German staff bus carrying valuable maps and documents.

Thanks in part to Lavrinenko's performance, the 4th Tank Brigade became the 1st Guards Tank Brigade in November 1941. Lavrinenko was promoted to Guards senior lieutenant. His platoon continued to fight on the approaches to Moscow. In part, Lavrinenko supported Major-General Ivan V. Panfilov's 316th Rifle Division on the Volokolamsk axis. His bold fighting style of rapid thrusts and surprise ambushes paid dividends, but it was a dangerous tactic. On 18 November 1941, Lavrinenko's tank was destroyed and the rest of his crew was killed. Lavrinenko himself escaped, but he could not cheat death forever. He was not killed in a tank duel, however, as would be likely for a tank ace. After successfully completing his mission on 18 December, he returned to Goryuny (modern-day Anino) to report his success to his brigade's commander. As he exited his tank, the village came under mortar fire; Lavrinenko was fatally wounded by a mortar shell splinter. He was buried in a mass grave located in Denkovo, Istra district.

In total, Lavrinenko's crews claimed 52 enemy tanks destroyed over 2½ months of combat, an exceptional result that was not surpassed by any other Soviet tank ace for the duration of the Great Patriotic War. Lavrinenko was nominated for the title of Hero of the Soviet Union on 5 December 1941; but the commander of the 16th Army, General Konstantin K. Rokossovsky, authorized only a lesser award, the Order of Lenin. The award was announced on 22 December, by which point Lavrinenko was already dead. The title of Hero of the Soviet Union was finally awarded to Lavrinenko by President Mikhail Gorbachev, nearly 50 years later on 5 May 1990.

manuals. Tank commanders who had not completed secondary education would attend night classes to make up for the missing curriculum. Tank commanders who had received secondary and post-secondary education would spend this time learning a foreign language.

Reservists could be called up for refresher training lasting two months (for privates) or three months (for privates training to become NCOs or NCOs training to become officers). This training could take place as often as annually for privates and NCOs under the age of 35 or junior officers under the age of 40; the age limit went up by five years for every two steps in rank to 60 for division commanders or their equivalents. Older men could still be called up for training, but only a handful of times. Reservists called up for training would retain their civilian jobs and receive half of their regular salary in addition to their Red Army pay.

THE STRATEGIC SITUATION

Drawn up in 1940, the German plan to invade the Soviet Union (Operation *Barbarossa*) took into account the Soviet Union's enormous size and relied on the rapid progress of armoured spearheads to encircle Red Army units stationed in the European part of the Soviet Union, prevent them from manoeuvring, and destroy them. The rapid progress of a significant force to such depth through the Soviet Union required a powerful tank arm.

Germany spent the better part of a decade developing such a force. The PzKpfw III finally took its intended place at the head of the *Panzerwaffe* by 22 June 1941. By this date, 1,440 PzKpfw III tanks were available for battle, 1,090 of which were the latest types armed with 5cm guns. They were joined by 517 PzKpfw IV medium tanks with similar armour and short 7.5cm guns, as well as 754 PzKpfw 38(t) light tanks produced in occupied Czechoslovakia. The PzKpfw 38(t)'s 50mm-thick frontal armour made it difficult to engage with the Soviet 45mm gun, while its 3.7cm gun could penetrate the armour of Soviet light tanks at long range. As far as German intelligence indicated, this was sufficient armament to take on any tank or armoured vehicle used by the Red Army. Also available were 160 PzKpfw 35(t) light tanks, less well armoured but armed with the same 3.7cm gun.

Older vehicles remained in German service: 337 PzKpfw I and 1,074 PzKpfw II light tanks were deployed to take part in Operation *Barbarossa*. The PzKpfw I was considered obsolescent and conversion into more useful vehicles, particularly the Panzerjäger I tank destroyer, had already started. The Czech 4.7cm KPÚV vz. 38 gun mounted on the Panzerjäger I was powerful enough to combat the T-34 successfully,

although the Germans did not know it yet. The same weapon was also installed on the chassis of captured French Renault R 35 tanks.

Confident that the Molotov–Ribbentrop Pact had bought him a few years of peace, Stalin turned to expanding the Red Army. A large part of this modernization consisted of a complete renewal of the tank fleet. The more common BT-7 and T-26 light tanks as well as the specialized T-28 medium and T-35 heavy tanks were declared obsolete and a multi-year production programme was undertaken to replace them. This was a slow process, however. In 1941, the Red Army was authorized to field 2,100 KV-1, 4,200 T-34, 8,273 BT, 15,872 T-26 and 3,681 T-37/-38 tanks in time of war; but projections showed that 1,093 KV-1 and 2,850 T-34 tanks – just 52 per cent and 67.8 per cent of the authorized strength respectively – could be delivered by 1 January 1942. Only 7,752 BT tanks and 9,987 T-26 tanks were available, which also fell short of wartime requirements. This figure would only decline as spare parts for these old types of tanks were not available in adequate quantities and no longer produced. The BT would eventually be replaced with the T-34, but the T-26's future was less certain. The new T-50 infantry-support tank was a good candidate to replace it, but only 500 such vehicles were ordered for 1941. At this pace, it would take until at least 1943 to prepare the Red Army for war.

The number of tanks available by 1 June 1941 was even smaller: 370 KV-1 and 134 KV-2 tanks joined 59 ageing T-35 tanks to make up a heavy-tank force less than one-quarter of the size that was required. Similarly, just 892 T-34 tanks were available, just over one-fifth of the required number. The bulk of the Red Army's tank fleet was made

A PzKpfw III moving to the front lines, July 1941. In the first weeks of the Axis invasion of the Soviet Union, the Germans could often move uncontested carrying infantry riders, as the Red Army had no idea where the Axis forces were. (SA-kuva)

Obstacle trials involving a typical T-34 in production by the end of 1941. (Tsentralniy Arkhiv Ministerstva Oborony Rossiyskoy Federatsii)

OPPOSITE

This map shows the German and Soviet formations equipped with either the PzKpfw III or the T-34 on the eve of Operation *Barbarossa*. On the German side, the following 11 *Panzer-Divisionen* fielded the PzKpfw III: 1. (71), 3. (110), 4. (105), 9. (71), 10. (105), 11. (71), 13. (71), 14. (71), 16. (71), 17. (106) and 18. (115). On the Soviet side, the following eight mechanized corps were equipped with the T-34: 2nd (50), 3rd (50), 4th (313), 6th (238), 8th (100), 11th (28), 15th (72) and 19th (9).

up of obsolete models. Of the 9,987 T-26 tanks on hand, 7,486 were traditional gun tanks; the rest consisted of outdated two-turret tanks armed only with machine guns as well as specialized vehicles such as remotely controlled unmanned teletanks and chemical tanks that would have little value in a tank-on-tank battle. Similarly, out of 7,752 BT tanks available, just 702 were the most advanced variant of the series, the BT-7M; 3,858 more were the older BT-7s, with the rest made up of outdated BT-5 or BT-2 light tanks.

It is also worth considering that the Soviet Union's armoured force was spread across the country's military districts and was not concentrated in the western areas to pre-empt a German invasion. Fewer than half of the Red Army's total number of tanks (12,223 gun tanks and 1,758 special vehicles) were present in western military districts, of which only 1,301 were T-34 or KV tanks.

The number of tanks available to the Red Army further dwindles when one considers their technical condition. Out of 13,981 AFVs stationed in border districts, only 2,157 were brand-new; 8,986 vehicles were used or in need of light repairs; and a further 2,838 were in need of serious repairs. The spare-parts shortage seriously depleted the latter category, and as much as 25 per cent of Soviet tanks in need of light repairs were not combat-capable due to missing tracks. A shortage of some 500,000 wheeled vehicles, 51,653 tractors and 69,691 trailers also meant that even where spare parts were available, they could not be delivered. A similar situation was observed with fuel and ammunition supplies. The defence of the Soviet Union was built on the idea that a small number of elite border units should be able to hold the line long enough for general mobilization to take place – an assumption that was to prove catastrophically wrong.

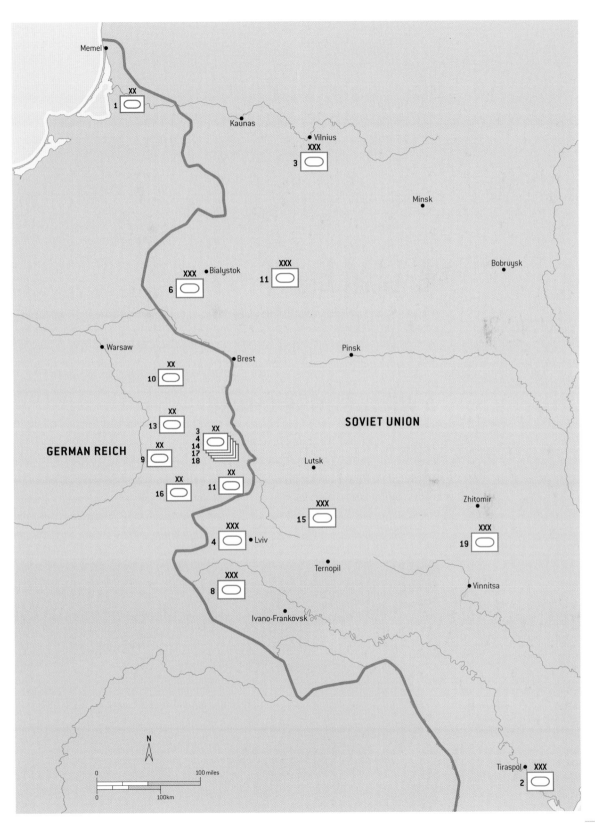

Memel

XX
1

Kaunas

Vilnius

XXX
3

Minsk

Bobruysk

XXX
6 Bialystok

XXX
11

Warsaw

Brest

Pinsk

XX
10

SOVIET UNION

XX
13

XX
3
4
14
17
18

GERMAN REICH

XX
9

Lutsk

XX
16

XX
11

XXX
15

Zhitomir

XXX
4 Lviv

XXX
19

Ternopil

XXX
8

Vinnitsa

Ivano-Frankovsk

N

0   100 miles

0   100km

Tiraspol

XXX
2

COMBAT

A WILD-GOOSE CHASE

Germany began final preparations for the invasion of the Soviet Union on the evening of 21 June 1941. Tank and mechanized formations replaced infantry stationed at the Soviet border. Just after midnight, small groups of German commandos crossed the border to prevent demolition of key bridges. As enemy movements on the other side of the border became of more and more concern, orders from Moscow stood firm: 'Do not fall for German provocation.' Some Soviet

PzBefWg III Ausf. H, Vadim Zadorozhny Technical Museum, Moscow. This was a command tank based on the PzKpfw III Ausf. H. The small 3.7cm gun is a dummy, the tank's only real weapon being a single 7.92mm MG 34 machine gun in a ball mount. (Author)

commanders gave orders to open the so-called 'red envelopes' regardless. These envelopes contained plans to deploy forces in border regions in order to establish a defence against an enemy vanguard. In practice, however, this meant very little. It took nine hours to execute those plans – nine hours that the Red Army simply did not have. It was also not the vanguard they would be facing, but the entire German invasion force.

Bombs and artillery shells began to fall on Soviet border installations at around 0400hrs. One hour later, Ribbentrop handed a diplomatic note with a declaration of war to the Soviet ambassador in Berlin, Vladimir G. Dekanozov. Around the same time, the German ambassador in Moscow, Friedrich Werner von der Schulenburg, was instructed to deliver a similar message to Molotov. At 0700hrs, Directive #2 signed by People's Commissar of Defence Semyon K. Timoshenko and Chief of the General Staff Georgy K. Zhukov finally permitted offensive action against German forces. It is unlikely that the border units that had already been fighting for three hours had ever seen the message.

At the border, chaos reigned. The 6th Mechanized Corps was deployed to intercept a German Panzer division at Bielsk (south of Białystok). The corps left its motorized infantry behind to protect the Narew River and began an arduous journey that ended up taking ten hours due to a complete lack of traffic organization. Considerable losses were taken from German air attacks, as large numbers of Soviet aircraft were destroyed on the ground in a series of surprise attacks at dawn on 22 June. The Germans now had complete control of the skies.

Having arrived at their destination, the 6th Mechanized Corps discovered that there were no German tanks at Bielsk. Efforts to gather delayed and disabled vehicles were interrupted by new orders to intercept the enemy between Grodno and Sokolka. No enemy tanks were found there either, but the Germans received yet another

PzKpfw III tanks from the 11. Panzer-Division advance across the steppe. With 1,440 Pz.Kpfw III tanks available to the *Panzerwaffe* in July 1941, the tank enjoyed a considerable numerical advantage over the T-34. (Arthur Grimm/ullstein bild via Getty Images)

German cavalry pass a T-34 and a T-26 flamethrower tank. It is possible that these tanks were lost without ever firing a shot, as Soviet tank forces were subjected to marches for days under a rain of German bombs without time to sleep, let alone conduct preventive maintenance to keep their tanks running. (Scherl/ Süddeutsche Zeitung Photo/ Alamy Stock Photo)

opportunity to bomb Red Army tank columns. To make matters worse, the 6th Mechanized Corps reported that they only had one-quarter load of fuel remaining – the fuel allocated to this corps was still held at a depot in Baranovichi, some 150km away. In addition, the corps reported that they had no ammunition. The 6th Mechanized Corps ceased to be a viable combat unit, essentially dissolving in the steppe as its subunits dashed from one phantom German tank unit to another under a rain of bombs.

The troops of the 8th Mechanized Corps found themselves in a similar situation. The corps was mobilized at 0540hrs on 22 June, moving out to Chyshky. At 2040hrs, while still en route, the corps was redirected to Kurovychi to counter an enemy attack at Brody, but by midday on 23 June the destination was changed yet again, this time to Yavoriv. The corps had a six-hour break before being sent to Busk, a journey that took nearly a full day due to the chaos on the roads. From Busk, the corps was redirected to Stanislavchik and Razhniv. As a result, the corps' tanks covered a distance of 495km on average without ever seeing the enemy. There was no time to conduct maintenance or get some sleep, as a result of which the corps left half of its tanks by the side of the road. The 12th Tank Division had a particularly rough time, as its drivers went for four days without sleep.

By the morning of 26 June, two-thirds of the 12th Tank Division's tanks had been abandoned. This was not due to design or manufacturing flaws but because the tanks were running for extended periods of time without preventive maintenance.

For example, regular maintenance of the V-2 engine included oiling it and cleaning the air filters every 50 hours of operation. (In peacetime, this procedure was performed after as little as 30 hours, but in the first days of the war the tanks could go for twice the maximum period without time even to clean the filters.) These pointless dashes back and forth without a clear objective had a devastating effect on the division's combat readiness. Tanks were abandoned due to minor and preventable mechanical issues, and even though they could have been evacuated and repaired relatively easily in optimal conditions, the odds of this happening in the chaos of late-June 1941 were slim.

The experience of the 6th and 8th Mechanized corps was not atypical. A report composed by the commander of the tank forces of the South-Western Front, Major-General Rodion N. Morgunov, painted a bleak picture of the first few days of fighting in his sector:

> In peacetime, a number of mechanized corps were located too close to the border. After the enemy's sudden attack, they couldn't be deployed forward, but had to retreat and then engage.
>
> Frequent and rushed changes in location ordered by superior staffs (70–80km away from the previous location in the span of one day) led to the units not being able to gather at the specified location and had to enter battle piecemeal. [...] A number of corps had to conduct 500km-long super-expedited marches in 3–4 days without keeping to elementary maintenance procedures and rest periods prescribed in manuals. As a result, 40–50% of the vehicles were out of action for technical reasons and the remaining materiel was not in a battle-ready condition. (TsAMO RF F.229 Op.157 D.8 L.217–29, quoted in Ulanov & Shein 2011: 228–29)

A PzKpfw III fording a river, July 1941. A portion of the fender is missing, suggesting that this tank had travelled over some rough ground. The usual section of spare tracks on the front is also missing, with only a small portion remaining on the turret platform front. (SA-kuva)

BORDER BATTLES

It would be inaccurate to say that T-34 tanks did not get to fight at all during the first days of the Great Patriotic War. An engagement took place between Generalmajor Ludwig Crüwell's 11. Panzer-Division and Major-General Sergei I. Ogurtsov's 10th Tank Division at Radekhiv. Crüwell's regiments fielded 45 PzKpfw II, 71 PzKpfw III, 20 PzKpfw IV and eight command tanks. The 11. Panzer-Division was formed in July 1940 and judged ready for service that October. Although the 15th Mechanized Corps to which the 10th Tank Division belonged began to form only in February 1941, Ogurtsov had a fair number of new tanks at his disposal. In total the 10th Tank Division had 63 KV, 37 T-34, 44 T-28, 147 BT-7 and 27 T-26 tanks.

As with the earlier border battles, chaos reigned. The 10th Tank Division was instructed to engage a German airborne landing force near Radekhiv and sent a small force consisting of two tank battalions to deal with it. Rather than facing a lightly armed group of paratroopers, however, the Soviet tankers were confronted with the 11. Panzer-Division as well as Kampfgruppe *Riebel* and Kampfgruppe *Angern*, which quickly swept aside the few Soviet tanks. In the meantime, German forward reconnaissance discovered the approach of the rest of the 10th Tank Division. The Germans laid an ambush, but it was not as effective as they had hoped. According to Unteroffizier Gustav Schrodek, a tank crewman of Panzer-Regiment 15: 'Despite repeated hits, our fire had no effect. It appears as if the shells are simply bouncing off. The enemy tanks disengaged without fighting and retreated' (quoted in Forczyk 2013: 110). This Red Army contingent was only an advance force. Ogurtsov was under orders to retake Radekhiv, and he was not about to give up this objective easily. He decided to attack the town, even though only one battalion from the 20th Tank Regiment and one battalion from the 10th Motorized Rifle Regiment had arrived, both without any artillery at all.

The 10th Tank Division's T-34 and KV-1 tanks opened fire on the Germans at a range of 800–1,000m, from which their 76mm guns easily defeated the armour of the PzKpfw III and PzKpfw IV tanks. Unfortunately for Ogurtsov, the Germans had brought more than just tanks; 8.8cm anti-aircraft guns from I./Flak-Regiment *General Göring* and heavy artillery of Artillerie-Regiment 119 were more than enough to penetrate even the thick armour of the new Soviet tanks. PzKpfw IV tanks also fired high-explosive shells in the hope of igniting fuel stored in the T-34's external fuel tanks.

The guns of the PzKpfw III and PzKpfw IV were more than enough to take on the Soviet light tanks that made up the majority of the 10th Tank Division's forces, and the Soviet attack petered out. The 10th Tank Division lost 46 tanks that day; but even if Ogurtsov's assault had proved successful, he would not have been able to hold the position for long. The 15th Mechanized Corps' riflemen were left far behind as they had to proceed to the border on foot; and the 37th Tank Division was sent six hours away to Adamovka to fight an enemy force that turned out to not have been there at all.

Another battle took place between the 5th Tank Division of the 3rd Mechanized Corps and the 7. Panzer-Division of the XXXIX. Armeekorps (mot.). In this instance, however, the Red Army had the advantage of knowing where the enemy was going to

Panzerkampfwagen Südwesteingang Radziechow

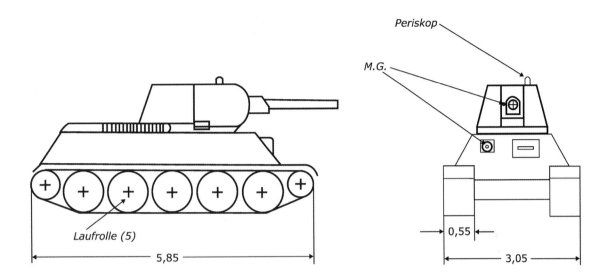

be. The 5th Tank Division was pulled out of its corps and attached directly to the 11th Army, which was ordered to hold bridges across the Neman River at the town of Alytus, some 50km from the Soviet–German border.

The 3rd Mechanized Corps was one of the better-equipped units of this type with a total of 672 tanks, 110 of which were the KV and T-34. Specifically, the 5th Tank Division had 50 T-34, 170 BT-7, 18 T-26 and 30 T-28 tanks plus 76 armoured cars. Even these tanks did not get to fight together, however, as the division was dispersed even further upon arrival. A battalion of motorized infantry supported by BA-10 armoured cars was sent to hold the Kaniūkai bridge south of Alytus. The 9th Tank Regiment, commanded by Colonel Ivan P. Verkov, was sent to hold the northern bridge going through Alytus itself.

Verkov's tanks were opposed by the 7. Panzer-Division of Panzergruppe 3, which fielded 17 PzKpfw I, 55 PzKpfw II, 30 PzKpfw IV and 174 PzKpfw 38(t) tanks plus 64 armoured cars. The German division also spread out when approaching Alytus. The northern bridge was attacked by Oberst Karl Rothenburg's Panzer-Regiment 25 supported by Panzer-Aufklärungs-Abteilung 37 and a group of flamethrower tanks.

Unfortunately for the Red Army, the Germans got to the bridges first. The 11th Army did not have the time to demolish the bridges to prevent the Germans' advance, nor to set up a proper echeloned defence. Panzer-Regiment 25 only came under attack when 20 tanks had already crossed to the eastern side. A T-34 tank in ambush easily destroyed one of the tanks and shrugged off return fire from 30 PzKpfw 38(t) tanks. The Soviet tank retreated, leaving the Germans a patch of land

Reproduction of an illustration accompanying a report compiled by the 297. Infanterie-Division regarding a new type of Soviet tank discovered on the south-western outskirts of Radekhiv, near the Bug River. The report incorrectly overestimates the weight of the tank at 35–40 tonnes, but this is unmistakably a T-34. (Author)

east of the bridge. The T-34s were able to hold them there. In particular, a T-34 tank commanded by Sergeant Makogon knocked out six German tanks that day, an impressive result considering that the 5th Tank Division had no 76mm armour-piercing shells. The division's 10th Tank Regiment, commanded by Colonel Terentiy Ya. Bogdanov, also engaged a battalion from Panzer-Regiment 25 and Oberst Carl-Hans Lungershausen's Schützen-Regiment 7. Five German tanks were destroyed as a result.

Despite having a numerical advantage in armour at Alytus, the Germans could not break through that day. Unfortunately, the lack of supporting infantry and artillery hampered the Soviet forces. Attempts to mount a counter-attack across the Neman without proper support resulted in Soviet losses, not so much from German tanks as from 10.5cm guns of Artillerie-Regiment 78. Elements of the 20. Panzer-Division that arrived by nightfall tipped the scales in the Germans' favour. Enough German tanks crossed the northern bridge to break out of the bridgehead and encircle the defenders on the southern flank. Alytus fell and the 5th Tank Division was forced to retreat.

Holding back a numerically superior force took a toll on the 5th Tank Division's armour: 73 tanks were left behind that day, including 27 T-34s out of the 44 that took part in the battle. The Germans also took significant losses. Only 11 tanks were written off completely, but the 7. Panzer-Division had no more than 150 operational tanks remaining after the battle and the II. Abteilung/Panzer-Regiment 25 (the same unit that first encountered the T-34s on the northern bridge) was disbanded. This was little consolation to the 5th Tank Division. Pursued by two German armoured divisions on its retreat to Vilnius, the Soviet division rapidly disintegrated into small groups of tanks acting on the initiative of junior officers.

Interestingly enough, Generaloberst Hermann Hoth took no note of the T-34 tanks his men encountered at Alytus. According to Hoth, the T-34 tanks first turned up during the crossing of the Berezina River at Barysaw in early July. Generaloberst Heinz Guderian, the commander of Panzergruppe 2, also recalled first seeing them here, even though photographic evidence suggests that his tankers had first encountered the T-34 in the earliest days of the Great Patriotic War. Some consider these to have been T-34 tanks attached to the 1st Moscow Proletarian Order of the Red Banner Motorized Rifle Division commanded by Colonel Yakov G. Kreizer. Interestingly enough, according to Kreizer's own memoirs, he did not receive any T-34 tanks until some time later, during the defence of Orsha.

Other German generals 'discovered' the T-34 much later. For example, Generalmajor Friedrich von Mellenthin mentions the appearance of T-34 tanks only in October. The presence of T-34 tanks was considered a formidable enough obstacle upon which to blame one's failures. The significance of T-34 tanks as a tactical threat was also felt by rank-and-file troops, who eagerly reported any enemy tank impeding their progress as being a T-34. Photographs of knocked-out tanks ranging from MS-1 (T-18) light tanks to Valentine infantry tanks with 'heavy Russian tank T-34' written on the back survive to this day. The Great Patriotic War was just beginning, however, and Guderian would get his fill of real T-34 tanks yet.

WEATHERING THE TYPHOON

The Stavka did not take long to react to the disastrous performance of the Red Army at the start of the Great Patriotic War. Upon reviewing the experience passed on by surviving tankers, mechanized corps were judged to be 'too massive, insufficiently mobile, clumsy, and ill-suited for manoeuvre, not to mention that they make easy targets for enemy aviation' (TsAMO RF F.48a Op.3408 D.4 L.1940–42, quoted in Ulanov & Shein 2011: 372). The surviving mechanized corps were dissolved into their composite divisions in mid-July 1941. The divisions themselves did not last long, however. By the end of August 1941, the Red Army began to form tank brigades instead of divisions, each consisting of just seven KV, 22 T-34 and 32 small or light tanks. The number of infantry was reduced to just one motorized rifle battalion.

The new formations arrived just in time for the Germans' renewed assault towards Moscow. After Operation *Barbarossa* failed to achieve its objectives, the

Germans organized a new thrust towards the Soviet capital codenamed Operation *Typhoon*. The plan called for a large-scale envelopment by three of the four *Panzergruppen*. In part, Guderian's Panzergruppe 2 (2. Panzerarmee as of 5 October 1941) was tasked with attacking from the south through Orel, Tula and Ryazan and finally linking up with Panzergruppe 1 east of Moscow. This was a distance of some 600km, comparable to what it took to get from the border to where Guderian's tanks stood at the end of September 1941, but the fighting ahead would be much more difficult. Instead of collapsing after the first blow as the Germans hoped, Red Army forces were bolstered by high morale and its commanders were eager to apply what they had learned during the first few months of defeat after defeat. One of the commanders was Colonel Mikhail Ye. Katukov, whose 4th Tank Brigade stood against Generalmajor Willibald von Langermann und Erlencamp's 4. Panzer-Division at Orel.

After breaking through the Soviet defences east of the Desna River on 30 September, Panzergruppe 2 split up. The XXXXVII. Panzerkorps turned north in order to close the Bryansk Pocket and General der Panzertruppe Leo Geyr von Schweppenburg's XXIV. Panzerkorps continued north-east towards Moscow. The commander of the Bryansk Front, Colonel-General Andrey I. Yeremenko, considered the XXXXVII. Panzerkorps to be the primary striking force, and thus dedicated relatively few resources to combating the XXIV. Panzerkorps.

At first, Schweppenburg moved at a brisk pace, covering the 240km distance to Orel in just four days. Realizing that Orel was under serious threat, the Stavka ordered the formation of the 1st Guards Rifle Corps under the command of Major-General Dmitry D. Lelyushenko on 2 October. Given that the XXIV. Panzerkorps was already in the vicinity of Orel by 3 October, Lelyushenko considered it senseless to throw the 1st Guards Rifle Corps at the Germans piecemeal. Instead, he decided to fight a delaying action and meet the Germans at a new line of defence at Mtsensk. The effect of the delay was significant, as it took another week for Schweppenburg to move a mere 35km from Orel to Mtsensk.

The 1st Guards Rifle Corps was a quite impressive formation. It included the 5th and 6th Guards Rifle divisions, 4th and 11th Tank brigades, 36th Motorcycle Regiment, a regiment of *Katyusha* multiple rocket launchers and two regiments-worth of anti-tank guns. The 4th Tank Brigade was the first to arrive, however, and took the greatest part in the delaying actions, as well as a significant part in the battle for Mtsensk itself.

On paper, Katukov's 4th Tank Brigade was a much weaker force than the pre-war tank divisions. It consisted of just seven KV-1, 22 T-34 and 26 BT-5 and BT-7 tanks, a battalion of 16 anti-aircraft guns, and technical support units. The brigade fought in a manner different from that of the tank divisions, however. This time, Soviet troops knew where the enemy was, where he was going, and how he was getting there. Reconnaissance groups from the brigade were sent to Orel on the night of 3/4 October as the core of the brigade arrived at Mtsensk, taking out targets of opportunity. Around Mtsensk, Katukov's troops built fake artillery positions that attracted the attention of German bombers. Soviet tankers ambushed and eliminated German reconnaissance elements, thereby denying the Germans detailed information about the nature of the real defences.

OPPOSITE

This map shows the fighting for
62   Mtsensk, 3–11 October 1941.

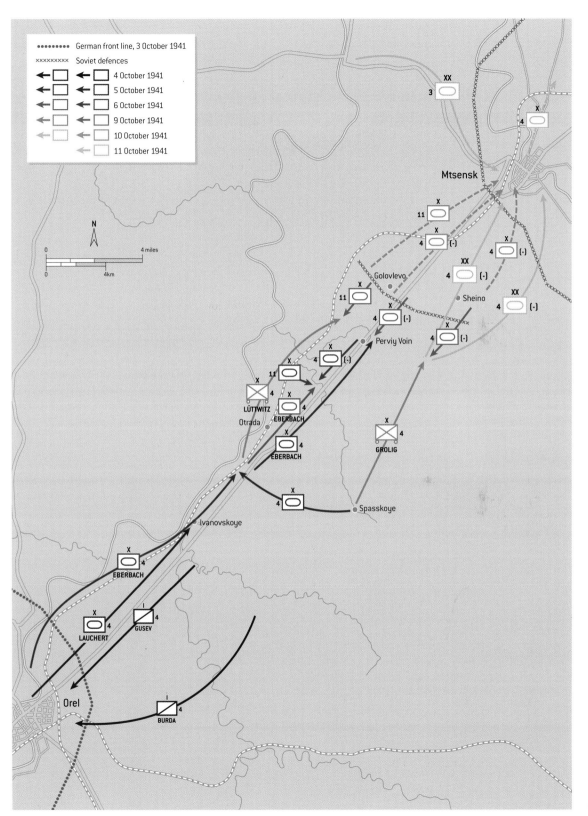

Katukov fought with bold, well-placed strikes. Tanks positioned in ambush positions along roads would destroy a German tank column, perform a shallow counter-attack and then quickly withdraw. The first such counterstroke was delivered on 4 October by a group led by Senior Lieutenant Alexandr F. Burda against a German vanguard. Larger German attacks that took place on 5 and 6 October were countered in the same way. Nevertheless, the area the 4th and 11th Tank brigades were tasked with defending was far too wide to protect forever. Despite weathering a much larger German attack on 9 October, Lelyushenko gave the order to withdraw to Mtsensk, because the Germans had broken through the Soviet lines nearby and threatened to encircle the 4th Tank Brigade.

Once again threatened with encirclement, Katukov's men and tanks stood their ground in front of Mtsensk, but the Germans broke through into the city from the south-east where the front was held by volunteer cadets from the Tula artillery school. The bulk of the 4th Tank Brigade retreated with only a small rearguard of six of the most trusted tank crews left behind. Crews led by Burda, Lieutenant Dmitry F. Lavrinenko, Senior Politruk Aleksandr S. Zagudayev, Lieutenant Grigoriy I. Timofeev, Sergeant Nikolai P. Kapotov and Captain Pavel A. Zaskalko roamed the city, using the brigade's favoured tactics of ambushes and bold short-range thrusts to delay the enemy. They also had a secondary mission: recovery of the brigade's disabled tanks.

At 0200hrs on 11 October the last of the 4th Tank Brigade's T-34 tanks crossed the Devil's Bridge with knocked-out tanks in tow, after which the bridge was demolished to cover their escape. Although Mtsensk fell, the performance of the brigade and its personnel was considered outstanding. The brigade was awarded the title of 1st Guards Tank Brigade and the aforementioned tankers received honours up to and including the title of Hero of the Soviet Union.

Even though the 4. Panzer-Division took Mtsensk, the German victory came at great cost. Panzer-Regiment 35 was down to 30 tanks out of 59 that were still in

Destroyed German vehicles including a PzKpfw III at Smolensk. German progress eastwards during Operation *Typhoon* was not as swift or bloodless as it was in the first months of the Great Patriotic War. (Starominskiy Istoriko-Krayevedcheskiy Muzey)

service on 4 October. The damage to vehicles not written off completely was severe enough that the 4. Panzer-Division was forced to stop its advance for two weeks in order to recover and refit. Red Army tank units also suffered significant losses. The 4th Tank Brigade lost 25 tanks, nine of which were written off and six could not be recovered from the battlefield. The 11th Tank Brigade lost 16 tanks on the approach to Mtsensk and during counter-attacks aimed at retaking the city.

As the once-rapid progress of the German armoured spearheads slowed, the advantages enjoyed by their opponents' tanks became more and more obvious. A report from Langermann und Erlencamp to Guderian read:

> In our battles, the 4. Panzer-Division often encountered Russian heavy tanks. At first they appeared rarely and could be stopped with concentrated artillery fire or bypassed. In some successful cases, lone heavy tanks were destroyed with a direct hit from artillery.
>
> After Orel was taken, the Russians first used heavy tanks en masse. There were cases of very heavy tank battles, as the Russians no longer allowed themselves to be stopped by artillery.
>
> For the first time during the war in the East, the absolute superiority of Russian 26- and 52-tonne tanks over our PzKpfw III and IV was felt.
>
> Russian tanks usually line up in a semicircle and open fire at our tanks at a distance of 1,000m using their 7.62cm guns that combine incredible penetration and high precision.
>
> [...]
>
> In addition to superior effectiveness of the armament and more powerful armour, the 26-tonne Christie tank (T-34) is faster and more manoeuvrable, its turret traverse mechanism has an obvious advantage. This tank's wide tracks allow it to ford rivers that our tanks cannot cross. The ground pressure is better than on our tanks, and despite the Russian tank's greater weight it can cross the same bridges that our tanks can.

T-34 and T-26 tanks stuck in a swamp outside of Talachyn between Minsk and Smolensk. These tanks were lost not in battle, but due to driving into an impassable swamp as a result of poor reconnaissance. (Tsentralniy Arkhiv Ministerstva Oborony Rossiyskoy Federatsii)

PzKpfw III GUNSIGHT VIEW

A PzKpfw III gunner aims at the side of a T-34 using his 2.4× TZF 5d telescopic gun sight. The PzKpfw III's 5cm gun could not reliably penetrate the front armour of a T-34 at any range, the only solution being to engage the T-34 from the side at close range. Several vehicles from the platoon would distract the T-34 while one or two crept up from the flanks where the T-34 commander, focused on the battle, would not see them coming.

T-34 GUNSIGHT VIEW

A T-34 gunner aims at a PzKpfw III platoon through his 2.5× TMFD-7 telescopic sight at a range of 2,000m. From here, he is guaranteed to score a killing shot while remaining well out of range of his opponents' 5cm guns.

The T-34's powerful V-2 engine allowed it to withdraw after firing well before the German tanks came into effective range.

The exceptional diesel engine also deserves attention. Not a single Russian tank left behind due to mechanical damage was found between Glebov and Minsk. To compare, Panzer-Regiment 35 alone left behind about 20 tanks on the way due to mechanical issues. Of course, we must remember that the Russian tanks are relatively new. (Quoted in Ulanov & Shein 2013: 160)

The report was not entirely negative, however. The officers of the 4. Panzer-Division were experienced soldiers and understood that any enemy has weaknesses. The report suggested installing a more powerful 5cm gun on the PzKpfw III, transplanting 76mm guns from captured T-34 tanks to the PzKpfw IV, as well as developing an anti-tank version of the 10.5cm field gun, which was effective against the T-34 but also large, heavy and very vulnerable. Despite offering these solutions, notes of panic began to creep through:

These facts and the impression that the Russians know about the technical supremacy of their armoured forces must be addressed in a timely manner in order to avoid damage done to our tank forces.

The energy and high spirit of our attacks will weaken and be lost due to a feeling of inadequacy. Crews know that enemy tanks can knock them out at a long range, but they can only have a minimal effect on enemy tanks despite the use of special ammunition at close range. (Quoted in Ulanov & Shein 2013: 161)

In his memoirs, Guderian gives the T-34 its due: 'The superiority of Russian T-34 tanks became evident for the first time. The [4. Panzer] division took heavy losses.

A T-34 leads a column of old-model light tanks towards the front lines, Moscow, November 1941. While the T-34 proved itself as one of the Red Army's most useful tanks, it would be a long time before it would make up the majority of the Red Army's armoured force. (Smolenskiy Gosudarstvenniy Muzey-Zapovednik)

The planned offensive towards Tula had to be delayed' (Guderian 1960: 212). The Germans treated the situation at Mtsensk very seriously. A commission headed by Ferdinand Porsche, the head of the Panzer Commission, arrived at Mtsensk to survey the battlefield and inspect captured weapons, especially T-34 tanks. This commission included a number of high-ranking figures: Oskar Hacker, Porsche's deputy and director of Steyr-Werke AG; Oberst Sebastian Fichtner, head of Wa Prüf 6; Heinrich Kniepkamp, the civilian head of Wa Prüf 6; and senior representatives of the leading arms companies Krupp, Daimler-Benz, Henschel, MAN and Rheinmetall. Officers present on the trip were impressed by the T-34 to the point of wanting a copy of it to be put into production in Germany. This was never done, as the industry representatives in the Panzer Commission estimated that a copy would take nearly as much time to put into production as a brand-new design. Nevertheless, various design elements of Soviet tanks were copied by German designers as a result of the Panzer Commission's work at Mtsensk.

Even though Katukov's blow made an impact on not just Guderian, but the whole Wehrmacht, it was just one tactical success on a very wide front. Nevertheless, Soviet tankers were getting a feel for their new tanks and their commanders were starting to learn what to do with them. These small successes became more and more frequent, and Operation *Typhoon* began to slip. Less than two months after the battle at Mtsensk, the German offensive ran out of steam and the Red Army launched a massive assault westward. The end of the Great Patriotic War was still far off, but the Red Army's armoured forces found their footing and showed that they were a worthy opponent to the German *Blitzkrieg*.

T-34 tanks in winter camouflage during the defence of Tula, winter 1941. (Archive PL/Alamy Stock Photo)

STATISTICS
AND ANALYSIS

It is difficult to describe Soviet losses in armour during the summer of 1941 as anything but staggering. As of 1 August, the Red Army had lost an estimated 1,303 T-34 tanks. As the Red Army found its footing, however, losses decreased. In the remaining five months of 1941, only 540 additional tanks were lost. Even though the fighting grew fiercer as the Germans neared Moscow, Soviet tankers were learning what their tanks and tank units were truly capable of, combined-arms commanders were learning how to support their tanks in combat with infantry and artillery, and technical personnel were learning how to recover and repair tanks in the chaos of battle. A shortage of technical personnel was a significant contributor to Soviet losses sustained in the early summer of 1941, as only 66 T-34 tanks were delivered to repair bases by 1 August; a tiny number compared to the number of broken tanks left behind German lines. Production barely kept up with T-34 losses, delivering 1,886 tanks between 1 July 1941 and 1 January 1942.

To put the losses in perspective, the Red Army's other new tank, the KV, was produced in much smaller numbers. The Red Army had about 500 KV-1 and KV-2 tanks on hand in June 1941 and 600 by December, having built almost 1,000 tanks in the interim. The majority of the Red Army's tank forces were still composed of light tanks, over 6,000 of which remained in service, both pre-war stock and newly produced examples of the T-60. This was still not enough. The Red Army needed another 2,997 KV-1, 7,541 T-34 and 5,747 T-50 or T-60 tanks in order to rebuild its strength. The GABTU estimated that this number of tanks

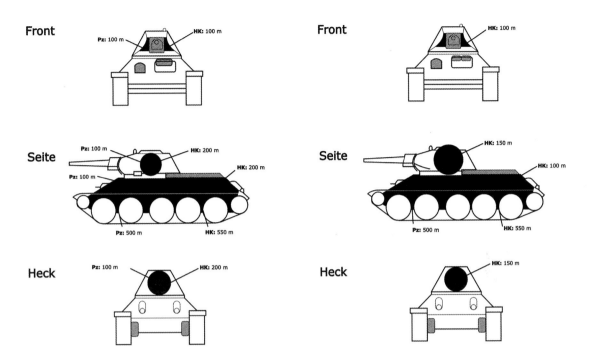

26-Tonner m PzKpfw T 34 A

Front

Pz: 100 m
HK: 100 m

Seite

Pz: 100 m
HK: 200 m
HK: 200 m
Pz: 100 m
Pz: 500 m
HK: 550 m

Heck

Pz: 100 m
HK: 200 m

26-Tonner m PzKpwf T 34 B (verstärkt)

Front

HK: 100 m

Seite

HK: 150 m
HK: 100 m
Pz: 500 m
HK: 550 m

Heck

HK: 150 m

could be provided in 10–11 months, not counting losses. For the time being, however, this shortfall had to be covered by light tanks alone. The T-34 would not become the Red Army's main tank until a conscious effort was made in the summer of 1942 to increase its production even at the cost of light- and heavy-tank output.

The Germans, who were able to recover and repair knocked-out vehicles, were in much better shape. Out of 1,440 PzKpfw III tanks available at the start of Operation *Barbarossa*, only 782 had been written off as permanent losses by the end of 1941. Unlike Soviet tank losses, however, the rate of German losses did not decrease as the Great Patriotic War wore on: 246 PzKpfw III tanks were written off by 1 August 1941, and 536 during the rest of the year. German industry was able to absorb the losses and the number of PzKpfw III tanks available increased to 1,849 by the end of 1941 out of a total of 4,896 tanks. The quantity of other German tanks only decreased. By the end of 1941, 513 PzKpfw IV tanks were still on the field, compared to 517 available at the start of Operation *Barbarossa*, with 348 having been written off. Only 381 PzKpfw 38(t) tanks remained compared to the 722 vehicles of this type available at the beginning of the invasion; 769 PzKpfw 38(t) tanks were destroyed during the second half of 1941, while 148 out of 189 PzKpfw 35(t) tanks were destroyed. As production at Škoda ended, it was impossible to replace them.

Fragment of a German instruction manual on fighting the regular T-34 and the 'reinforced' T-34 (likely referring to later-model tanks with cast turret armour). Solid black indicates areas where the T-34 can be penetrated with regular armour-piercing ammunition and tungsten-carbide sub-calibre shot. Hatched areas indicate areas that should be shot at with high-explosive shells to degrade the performance of the T-34. The PzKpfw III's gunner had very few options when engaging a T-34 outside of suicidal close range, unless he managed to score a hit on its lower hull from the side. (Author)

While Soviet losses were considerably greater in the summer of 1941, the tide began to turn at the end of the year. German forces reported a total loss of 506 tanks (including 208 PzKpfw III) and 19 *Sturmgeschützen* in December 1941. The number of German tanks available for battle dropped even more, from 4,084 to 2,758. To compare, Soviet tank losses in operations that took place in December 1941 numbered 541 vehicles. These figures only give an approximate impression of losses in armoured vehicles, however, as the strategic operations in question do not precisely line up with calendar months (for example, the Tikhvin Offensive Operation lasted from 11 November to 30 December). The figures for German tanks also omit all foreign and captured tanks with the exception of the PzKpfw 38(t) and self-propelled guns on tracked and half-tracked chassis. Writing off a vehicle as a total loss also did not necessarily take place as soon as it was destroyed, so the total for December could include tanks from the end of November and likewise omit tanks lost at the very end of December. Nevertheless, the order of magnitude of the losses was comparable for both sides.

The high rate of Soviet tank losses is often attributed to the superior designs of German tanks, and yet analysis of figures shows otherwise. The T-34 and PzKpfw III tanks that clashed at the border in late-June 1941 were exactly the same tanks as those that met at Mtsensk or at Moscow. There were no changes made to the T-34 that bolstered its fighting ability, nor some deficiency introduced into the PzKpfw III that reduced its effectiveness. Likewise, the claim that the Red Army won due to superiority in numbers alone does not stand up to scrutiny, as the number of PzKpfw III tanks only grew while the number of T-34 tanks on the battlefield remained approximately the same. By the start of 1942, the PzKpfw III outnumbered the T-34 nearly 2:1. If the quality of tanks was the only factor that decided the outcome of a battle, then the Germans would have broken through the Red Army tank brigades guarding Moscow as easily as they had the mechanized corps at the border. The Germans' reversal of fortune in December 1941 had nothing to do with the technical specifications of any type of tank, but the growing skill of Soviet commanders.

That is not to say that German commanders passively stood by as their opponent grew in strength. In addition to using heavy artillery including 8.8cm and 10.5cm towed guns to combat the T-34, sophisticated tactics were developed to allow German medium tanks to combat the T-34 despite having thinner armour and a weaker gun. Letter #126/42, sent by the OKH on 26 May 1942, demonstrates both an appreciation of the T-34's abilities and an understanding that there is no such thing as a tank without weaknesses:

Tactics of Russian tanks:
In defence and during retreating battles, the T-34 tanks are dug in including the turret on dominating heights, near roads, in forest clearings and in settlements in such a way that after a quick artillery barrage it can retreat. Knowing its superiority in armament, the T-34 opens fire at attacking tanks from 1200–1800 metres. Since the T-34 is faster than the German tanks, it can choose the engagement distance.
Tactics of our tanks:
Since it is only possible to penetrate the T-34 from the flanks from a short distance with the 50mm gun, the correct way to engage T-34 tanks is with the following tactics:

VULNERABLE AREAS OF THE
GERMAN T-III TANK

Brief data
1. Armour: front, sides, and turret: 30-40 mm
2. Engine: gasoline
3. Length: 5.4 m, width: 2.9 m height: 2.5 m
4. Armament: 37-mm or 50-mm cannon and 2 machine guns

Translation of a Soviet pamphlet detailing the weaknesses of the PzKpfw III. While the PzKpfw III was vulnerable to 57mm and 76mm guns at essentially any range, these weapons were relatively rare in 1941. The latest PzKpfw III Ausf. J tanks with up to 50mm of armour were decently protected against every other weapon in the Soviet arsenal. (Author)

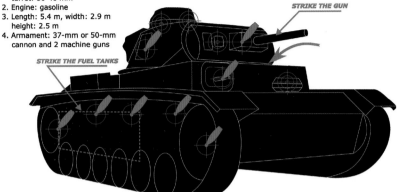

STRIKE THE GUN

STRIKE THE FUEL TANKS

VULNERABLE RANGES

1. 45-mm gun at ranges of 200 m.
2. 57-mm and 76-mm guns at all ranges of aimed fire.
3. Anti-tank rifle at ranges of 150-200 m.
4. Heavy machine gun aimed at sides, observation slits, and armament at all ranges of aimed fire.
5. Molotov Cocktails at ranges of 15-20 m.
6. Anti-tank grenades at ranges of 15-20 m.

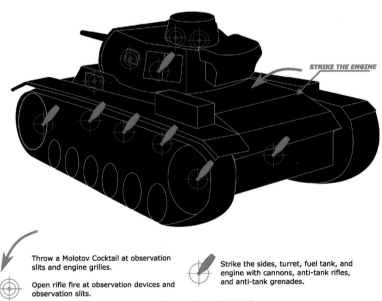

STRIKE THE ENGINE

Throw a Molotov Cocktail at observation slits and engine grilles.

Open rifle fire at observation devices and observation slits.

Strike the sides, turret, fuel tank, and engine with cannons, anti-tank rifles, and anti-tank grenades.

Military publisher USSR NKO
Moscow - 1942   Pravda newspaper typography order 1923

1. Tie up the tank with three Pz.III tanks that engage in a firefight. Taking up positions on a reverse slope or moving constantly will make it harder to engage the enemy.

2. Meanwhile, two more Pz.III tanks using all cover rush to the T-34 from the left and right flanks or come in from the rear and fire from a short distance using Pz.Gr.40 shot, aiming for the sides or the rear of the tank.

3. If there is a Pz.IV among our tanks, it is used to tie up the T-34 from the front. Using a smokescreen, the Pz.IV can blind the T-34 or cover the approach of other tanks. It is likely that the enemy will mistake the smoke for chemical weapons and disengage on its own.

When meeting tanks that are superior in quality and quantity to our own tanks (T-34 and KV), success is obtained only if the entire tank unit forms a single front of fire and blinds the enemy with fire. Even if not a single tank was knocked out, the enemy still almost always disengaged under the precision and speed of German tank fire. (TsAMO RF F.3181 Op.1 D.6 L.44)

German infantry was also quite concerned about facing the T-34. Extensive experiments were carried out to develop tactics ranging from ingenious to suicidal. German manuals suggested 'blinding' a T-34 by wrapping two smoke grenades tied together with string around the gun barrel. Particularly brave soldiers could climb up on the tank with a bucket of mud and cover up the viewports, although the manual did not describe what to do if the tank was in motion. Other tactics, such as breaking open the engine grille with an axe and throwing a grenade inside or pouring a canister of petrol inside, were just as risky. All of these methods required perfect knowledge of the T-34's blind spots, a steel will and a good amount of luck to carry out. Eike Middeldorf, a staff officer of the 4. Panzer-Division and future Bundeswehr *Generalmajor*, wrote:

The path of suffering of German infantry against Russian T-34 tanks is drawn from the 37mm gun that the Army called 'door knocker', through a 50mm gun, and to the mechanized 75mm gun. Perhaps it will never be known why in the 3½ years since the first appearance of the T-34 in August of 1941 and until April of 1945 an acceptable anti-tank weapon for the infantry was not created. (Middeldorf 2000: 16)

AFTERMATH

While the Red Army's organization required drastic changes, the armour and armament of the T-34 proved themselves in battle in 1941. Barring small batches of tanks given appliqué armour, the T-34 retained the same level of protection until production ceased in 1944. The 76mm F-34 gun was also found to be sufficient. The 57mm ZIS-4 gun in development was cancelled, and the F-34 and ZIS-5 (which had equivalent ballistics) remained as the primary weapons of Soviet medium and heavy tanks until 1943, when they were found to be unsatisfactory in trials against the Tiger tank.

A 1942-production T-34, Patriot Park. As the T-34's armour and firepower were generally satisfactory, most changes made after 1941 were aimed at simplifying production. What used to be a disjointed group of factories each working under a different People's Commissar was brought together under one NKTP (People's Commissariat of Tank Production), capable of organizing the evacuating tank factories into a series of powerful industrial centres, including the legendary Tankograd ('Tank City', Chelyabinsk). These new factories answered to only one boss, making it much easier to organize the production of tanks in sufficient quantities to rebuild the Red Army's depleted tank fleet. Direct control over the factories also made it that much easier to propagate design changes and ensure high-quality output. (Author)

PzKpfw III Ausf. N, The Tank Museum, Bovington. Because the PzKpfw III could not accommodate a high-velocity gun to compete with contemporary Soviet tanks, the Ausf. N was repurposed for close-support duty and received the same low-velocity 7.5cm KwK L/24 that the PzKpfw IV had, while the PzKpfw IV became the new main medium tank. (Author)

Attempts were made to remedy other aspects of the T-34. In 1942 the T-34S, with an improved five-speed transmission, third turret crewman and commander's cupola, entered trials and a transmission with a five-speed gearbox was put into production. In 1943 a commander's cupola entered production and the T-34-85, with a three-man turret and 85mm D-5T gun, was accepted into service. Medium tanks were now commanded only by officers and crewed by NCOs, with a senior lieutenant commanding a medium-tank platoon and a captain commanding a company.

The Germans faced different challenges. Their tactics and organization worked well enough, but the armour and armament of their tanks was found to be lacking. Production of a PzKpfw III armed with a longer 5cm gun began by the end of 1941, but even this was insufficient. A long-barrelled 7.5cm gun was required to combat the T-34 and KV-1. Such a gun could fit in a PzKpfw IV without considerable design changes, but not in a PzKpfw III, leading to its replacement.

The armour of the PzKpfw III was also augmented. Spaced armour in front of the turret platform and gun shield offered some protection against the T-34's 76mm gun, but the plates and the bolts holding them in place cracked and broke off when hit. *Schürzen* (spaced armour) introduced in 1943 to protect the sides was only effective against anti-tank rifles. In short, the encounters with the T-34 in the summer of 1941 marked the beginning of the end for the PzKpfw III. Production of the PzKpfw III tapered off and ceased in August 1943, although existing tanks and special vehicles built on their chassis continued to fight until the end of the Great Patriotic War.

BIBLIOGRAPHY

Primary sources

RGAE: *Rossiyskiy Gosudarstvenniy Arkhiv Economiki*, Russian State Economics Archive.

RGVA: *Rossiyskiy Gosudarstvennyi Voyenny Arkhiv*, Russian State Military Archive.

TsAMO RF: *Tsentral'nyy Arkhiv Ministerstva Oborony Rossiyskoy Federatsii*, Central Archive of the Ministry of Defence of the Russian Federation.

RGAE F.7515 Op.1 D.231 L.136–37, *Prikaz Narodnogo Kommissara Oboronnoy Promyshlennosti #337ss.*

RGAE F.7914 Op.1 D.26 L.1–19, *Postanovleniye #443 Komiteta Oborony pri SNK Soyuza SSR.*

RGAE F.8752 Op.4 D.83 L.174, *Prikaz po Narkomatu tankovoy promyshlennosti #206-ms.*

RGVA F.4 Op.18 D.46 L.259–71, *Protokol #28 zasedaniya GVS RKKA.*

RGVA F.4 Op.19 D.55 pp.1-9, letter #3 from ABTU Chief Pavlov to People's Commissar of Defence Voroshilov.

RGVA F.31811 Op.2 D.842 L.21–36, *Taktichesko-tekhnicheskiye trebovaniya na proyektirovaniye tanka proryva.*

RGVA F.31811 Op.2 D.842 L.263–315, *Obyasnitelnaya zapiska k tekhnicheskomu proyektu tanka A-20 i A-20 gus.*

RGVA F.31811 Op.2 D.888 L.49, letter #53ss from ABTU Military Representative Dmitrusenko to ABTU Chief Pavlov.

RGVA F.31811 Op.2 D.1130 L.67–79, *Otchet #027 ot 28 sentyabrya 1940 g po voprosu polevykh ispytaniy radiooborudovaniya mashin A-34.*

RGVA F.31811 Op.2 D.1130 L.175–78, *Protokol #030 ot 22.10.40.*

RGVA F.31811 Op.2 D.1181 L.133, letter #73965s from ABTU Chief Fedorenko to factory #183 management.

RGVA F.31811 Op.2 D.1182 L.89–90, *Otchet po ispytaniyu tryekh tankov T-34 dlitelnym probegom.*

RGVA F.31811 Op.3 D.974 L.1–17, *Taktichesko-tekhnicheskiye trebovaniya na proyektirovaniye i izgotovleniye lyogkogo kolesno-gusenichnogo bystrokhodnogo tanka BT-20.*

RGVA F.31811 Op.3 D.1633 L.16–19, *Programma poligonnykh ispytaniy opytnykh tankov A-20, A-32 v letnikh usloviyakh.*

RGVA F.31811 Op.3 D.1633 L.111–13, *Svodka o khode opytnykh rabot na zavode 183 po sostoyaniyu na 6.7.39 g.*

RGVA F.31811 Op.3 D.1850 L.1–90, *Tekhnicheskiye usloviya na sborku i priyemku mekhanizmov i ispytaniye mashiny A-34 vypuska 1940 g.*

RGVA F.31811 Op.3 D.2116 L.1–100, *Otchet po ispytaniyu tryekh tankov T-34 dlitelnym probegom.*

TsAMO RF F.33 Op.682524 D.240 L.3, *Ukaz prezidiuma verkhovnogo soveta SSSR o nagrazhdenii ordenami i medalyami nachalstvuyeshego i ryadovogo sostava Krasnoy Armii.*

TsAMO RF F.38 Op.11355 D.6 L.199–200, *Taktichesko-tekhnicheskaya kharakteristika tanka A-20.*

TsAMO RF F.38 Op.11355 D.41 L.10–11, letter #SO6913 from Chief Engineer at factory #183 Makhonin to GABTU Military Representative Kozyrev.

TsAMO RF F.38 Op.11355 D.49, *Postanovleniye SNK i TsK VKP(b) o postavke zavodami promyshlennosti zapasnykh chastey, agregatov, i eletrkrooboruduvaniya k tankam.*

TsAMO RF F.38 Op.11355 D.178 L.1–20, *Otchet po ispytaniyu opytnykh obraztsov smotrovogo pribora voditelya, boyeukladki, sideniy komandira i zaryazhayushego tanka T-34.*

TsAMO RF F.38 Op.11355 D.232 L.29, letter #SO364 from Chief Engineer at factory #183 Makhonin to GABTU Military Representative Kozyrev and BTU Chief Alymov.

TsAMO RF F.38 Op.11355 D.778, *Otchet TsNII-48 po teme: izucheniye bronevoy zaschity tankov nemetskoy armii.*

TsAMO RF F.38 Op.11355 D.804 L.19, *Preodoleniye snezhnykh valov nemetskim tankom T-3.*

TsAMO RF F.38 Op.11355 D.817, *Otchet NIP GABTU KA po sravnitelnym ispytaniyam importnykh i trofeynykh tankov.*

TsAMO RF F.38 Op.11355 D.832, *Otchet NIBT poligona po ispytaniyu nemetskikh tankov obstrelom broneboynimi i oskolochnimi snaryadami iz tankovykh pushek.*

TsAMO RF F.38 Op.11355 D.958 L.18, letter #2912ss from Marshal Kulik and GABTU Chief Fedorenko to the Central Committee of the VKP(b).

TsAMO RF F.38 Op.11355 D.1712 L.93, letter from Red Army GRU Chief Ilyichev to the Commander of the Red Army Armoured and Mechanized Forces Fedorenko.

TsAMO RF F.48a Op.1551 D.91 L.311–312, *Direktiva Stavki VGK #002517.*

TsAMO RF F.202 Op.50 D.42 L.95, German document on penetration of French vehicles captured in the region of the Vysokoye village, 52km north of West Livna.

TsAMO RF F.3181 Op.1 D.6 L.44, *Nastvleniye po borbe nashikh tankov s russkim tankom T-34.*

H.Dv. 469/3b Panzerabwehr aller Waffen (All. Pz. Abw.) Heft 3b Panzer-Beschusstafel (Abwehr schwer zu bekämpfender Panzerfahrzeuge) Panzer.

Anlage zu H.Dv.469/3b Panzer-Beschußtafel (Abwehr schwer zu bekämpfender Panzerfahrzeuge) 5cm KwK 39 5cm KwK 39/1 u. 5cm KwK 39/2.

H.Dv. 470/1 Ausbildungsvorschrift für die Panzertruppe (A.V. Pz.) Heft 1 A. Leitsätze für die Erziehung und Ausbildung im Heere. B. Ausbildungsziele für die Einzelausbildung der Panzertruppe.

Canadian Military Headquarters, London (CMHQ), Files Block No. 55-5776, image 1922, Proposal for All-Round Vision Cupola from the Medical Research Council and Army Operations Research Group Laboratories, Lulworth, Appendix 6.

Canadian Military Headquarters, London (CMHQ), Files Block No. 55-5788, image 3336, *Thickness against critical velocity for perforation, German 5cm APC Shell (welded head) v. Homogenous Plate.*

Evaluation Report No.153 Combined Intelligence Objectives Sub-committee, Interrogation of Herr Stiele von Heydekampf Target Nos. 18/2 19/7, 19/71, Digital History Archive.

Weisung Nr. 21 'Fall Barbarossa', 18. Dezember 1940, 100(0) Schlüsseldokumente zur Deutschen Geschichte im 20. Jahrhundert.

Publications

Anonymous (1944). *Preliminary Report No.20 Russian T/34.* Chertsey: Military College of Science, School of Tank Technology.

Baryatinskiy, M. (2012). *Sovetskiye tankoviye asy.* Moscow: Yauza.

Dinaro, R. (2006). *Germany's Panzer Arm in World War II.* Mechanicsburg, PA: Stackpole Books.

Dorogovoz, I. (2003). *Tankoviy Mech Strany Sovetov.* Minsk: Harvest.

Drig, Ye. (2005). *Mekhanizirovanniye korpusa RKKA v boyu: Istoria avtobronetankovykh voysk Krasnoy Armii v 1940–1941 godakh.* Moscow: Ast.

Forczyk, R. (2013). *Tank Warfare on the Eastern Front 1941–1942: Schwerpunkt.* Barnsley: Pen & Sword.

Goryushin, N., Chufaroiskiy, V., Kotshir, S. & Sytin, B. (1944). *Tank T-34 Rukovodstvo.* 2nd edition. Moscow: Voyenizdat.

Guderian, H. (1960). *Erinnerungen eines Soldaten.* Neckargemünd: Kurt Vowinckel Verlag.

Hoth, H. (1956). *Panzer-Operationen.* Heidelberg: Kurt Vowinckel Verlag.

Isayev, A. (2004). *Antisuvorov.* Moscow: Eksmo.

Isayev, A. (2010). *Neizvestniy 1941. Ostanovlenniy Blitzkrig.* Moscow: Eksmo.

Krivosheev, G. (2009). *Velikaya Otechestvennaya bez grifa sekretnosti. Kniga poter.* Moscow: Veche.

Michaelis, C. (2020). *Rüstungsmanagement der Ministerien Todt und Speer. Das Beispiel Panzerentwicklung/Panzerkommission.* Münster: Aschendorff Verlag.

Middeldorf, E. (2000). *Russkaya kampaniya: taktika i vooruzheniye.* St Petersburg: AST.

Mitcham Jr., S. (2006). *The Panzer Legions: A Guide to the German Army Tank Divisions of World War II and Their Commanders.* Mechanicsburg, PA: Stackpole Books.

Mueller-Hillebrand, B. (1950). *German Tank Losses.* Versailles: Historical Division European Command Operational History Branch.

Operational Research Directorate of the General Staff of the Armed Forces of the USSR (1950). *Sbornik boyevykh dokumentov Velikoy Otechestvennoy voiny*, Vol. 10. Moscow: Voyenizdat.

Orlovskiy, M. (2007). *Sredniy tank Pz.III Sd.Kfz.141.* Moscow: Tseikhgauz.

Shtrom, I.V. (1941). *Rukovodstvo po obucheniyu vozhdeniyu tankov.* Moscow: Voyenizdat.

Steiger, R. (1973). *Panzertaktik im Spiegel deutscher Kriegstagebücher 1939 bis 1941.* Freiburg: Rombach & Co. GmbH.

Tolokonnikov, L. (1944). *Nablyudeniye iz sovremennykh tankov, Vestnik Bronetankovoy Promyshlennosti #10 1944.* Moscow: Voyenizidat.

Ulanov, A. & Shein, D. (2011). *Poryadok v takhovykh voyskakh.* Moscow: Veche.

Ulanov, A. & Shein, D. (2013). *Perviye Tridtsatchetverki.* Moscow: Tactical Press.

US War Department (1945). *Handbook on German Military Forces.* War Department Technical Manual TM-E 30-451.

Zaloga, S.J. (2017). *Panzer 38(t) vs BT-7: Barbarossa 1941.* Duel 78. Oxford: Osprey Publishing.

Zheltov, I. & Makarov, A. (2014). *A-34 Rozhdeniye Tridtsatchetverki.* Moscow: Tactical Press.

Websites

Drabkin, A. *Bauer Ludwig*, https://frontstory.ru/memoirs/germany/bauer-ludwig/ (retrieved 4 March 2023).

Makarov, A. *Sredniy Tank T-34. Razvitiye Bronevoy Zaschity v 1939-1943 gg*, https://www.youtube.com/watch?v=1wgW4bces7E (retrieved 27 February 2023).

Makarov, A. & Zheltov, I. *Nachalo osvoyeniya seriynogo proizvodstva tankov T-34*, https://t34inform.ru/publication/p03-3.html (retrieved 27 February 2023).

Nevskiy, N. *Pod znakom srednego tanka*, https://warspot.ru/4621-pod-znakom-srednego-tanka (retrieved 5 March 2023).

Nevskiy, N. *Rozhdyenniy voynoy. Kak sozdavalsya narkomat tankovoy promyshlennosti*, https://warspot.ru/3889-rozhdyonnyy-voynoy-kak-sozdavalsya-narkomat-tankovoy-promyshlennosti (retrieved 5 March 2023).

Pasholok, Y. *Bystrokhodniy tank po-nemetski*, https://warspot.ru/5911-bystrohodnyy-tank-po-nemetski (retrieved 2 March 2023).

Pasholok, Y. *Nemetskaya rabochaya loshadka serediny voyny*, https://dzen.ru/a/YFum1myMHldfzuct (retrieved 2 March 2023).

Pasholok, Y. *Perekhodnaya Troyka*, https://warspot.ru/11139-perehodnaya-troyka (retrieved 2 March 2023).

Pasholok, Y. *Perviy massoviy nemetskiy serednyak*, https://warspot.ru/10614-pervyy-massovyy-nemetskiy-serednyak (retrieved 2 March 2023).

Pasholok, Y. *Posledniye modifikatsii troyki*, https://warspot.ru/11613-poslednie-modifikatsii-troyki (retrieved 2 March 2023).

Pasholok, Y. *Promezhutochnoye zveno v treshechnom semeystve*, https://dzen.ru/a/X3bvk39ya2o5fNUl (retrieved 2 March 2023).

Pasholok, Y. *Snegokhodniye svoystva tankov zimoy 1941-42 godov*, https://dzen.ru/a/X-mXwNuh60r4pYPp (retrieved 2 March 2023).

Pasholok, Y. *Surprizy na snegu*, https://dzen.ru/a/X_RVhq8ULwsX-kOx (retrieved 2 March 2023).

Pasholok, Y. *Troyki na ressorakh*, https://warspot.ru/6871-troyki-na-ressorah (retrieved 2 March 2023).

Samsonov, P. *Kak ubit tridtsatchetverku*, https://warspot.ru/20942-kak-ubit-tridtsatchetvyorku (retrieved 2 March 2023).

Samsonov, P. *Tridtsatchetverka na gastrolyakh*, https://warspot.ru/13725-tridtsatchyotverka-na-gastrolyah (retrieved 2 March 2023).

Smirnov, A. *Tankoviy as Dmitry Lavrinenko*, http://armor.kiev.ua/Battle/WWII/lavrinenko/ (retrieved 4 March 2023).

Tarasenko, A. *Posledniy ekzamen serdtsa tridtsatchetverki*, https://warspot.ru/6951-posledniy-ekzamen-serdtsa-tridtsatchetvyorki (retrieved 5 March 2023).

Zaitsev, D. *T-34 i nemtsy*, https://warspot.ru/7378-t-34-i-nemtsy (retrieved 5 March 2023).

4-ya tankovaya brigada, http://www.tankfront.ru/ussr/tbr/tbr004.html (retrieved 4 March 2023).

Lavrinenko Dmitry Fedorovich, https://pamyat-naroda.ru/heroes/person-hero109028887/ (retrieved 4 March 2023).

INDEX

References to illustrations are shown in **bold**.